MORE ABOUT
EGYPTIAN HIEROGLYPHS

FOR JUAN AND JUANA

MORE ABOUT
EGYPTIAN HIEROGLYPHS

A simplified grammar of Middle Egyptian

BY

BARBARA WATTERSON

SCOTTISH ACADEMIC PRESS

EDINBURGH

Published by
Scottish Academic Press Ltd.
33 Montgomery Street, Edinburgh EH7 5JX

ISBN 0 7073 0362 1

British Library Cataloguing in Publication Data

Watterson, Barbara
  More about Egyptian hieroglyphs.
  1. Egyptian language—Writing, Hieroglyphic
  I. Title
  493'.1   PJ1097

ISBN 0-7073-0362-1

Printed in Great Britain by
Page Bros (Norwich) Ltd

CONTENTS

Contents

INTRODUCTION

'More About Egyptian Hieroglyphs' is a sequel to the author's 'Introducing Egyptian Hieroglyphs' (Scottish Academic Press, 1981) in which chapters on the origin and nature of the script and language of the Ancient Egyptians, and the history of the decipherment of hieroglyphs, provided an introduction to a series of eleven lessons which aimed to give the reader enough basic grammar and vocabulary for him to be able to attempt the translation of simple hieroglyphic inscriptions.

'More About Egyptian Hieroglyphs' is an attempt to bring a simplified grammar of the Ancient Egyptian language to the lay or professional student in the form of a practical manual in which aspects of the Egyptian language are dealt with in twenty chapters, in each of which grammatical points are explained by first illustrating their use in terms of English grammar. At the end of each chapter, the reader's understanding of the points is 'tested' by means of an exercise, the key to which is provided at the end of the book, as are English-Egyptian and Egyptian-English vocabularies for the exercises.

Readers with a sound technical grasp of English grammar will find some sections unnecessary, perhaps irritatingly so! However, experience has shown that a familiarity with grammatical structure, analysis and nomenclature is by no means universal even amongst language students, and I am confident that some readers will be grateful for that which the savant may disdain. Although the reader with some prior knowledge of Middle Egyptian will be able to use 'More About Egyptian Hieroglyphs' on its own, ideally it should be read in conjunction with 'Introducing Egyptian Hieroglyphs', to which references are made throughout the present work.

It is hoped that neither book will give the reader the impression that Ancient Egyptian is a language whose simplicity is disguised only by the use of picture writing; or that modern scholars have solved all the grammatical problems connected with it; or, indeed, are unanimous in acceptance of the solutions proposed for some of these problems. This is very far from being the case, and anyone who studies Sir Alan Gardiner's 'Egyptian Grammar', still the classic work for English-speaking students even though it was first published nearly fifty years ago, will be rapidly disabused of such a notion.

Several grammars of the various stages of the Egyptian language have been published in the last few years, although none as yet has superceded Gardiner's work on Middle Egyptian. However, they tend to be written in a scholarly, sometimes esoteric, way that is perhaps a little too specialized for those who are interested in the Egyptian language but who lack the formal linguistic background that such books assume.

Having mastered the framework of Egyptian grammar as set out in 'More About Egyptian Hieroglyphs', the reader may then turn to Gardiner with profit, since Gardiner will furnish him with an exhaustive supply of information about Egyptian syntax, and with a source of reference for the many variant writings of verbs, participles and other words.

Eventually, most readers will want to put into practice what they have learned. Those fortunate enough to be able to visit Egypt will be able to try out their newly-acquired knowledge of Ancient Egyptian by endeavouring to translate inscriptions on the walls of temples and tombs; otherwise, a visit to any museum with an Egyptian collection will enable them to study inscriptions on statue bases, coffins, reliefs, funerary stelae, and so on; and many people will have access to a 'Cleopatra's Needle', since over fifty of these obelisks are to be found in public parks all over the world.

At first, attempts to translate hieroglyphic inscriptions will be discouraging for many people: hieroglyphs can look very different in real life from the way they look in books, for simple practical reasons such as their position on a wall or column, or their incompleteness due to damage or to erosion by weathering. A degree of persistence is therefore essential so that, gradually, the clichés employed by the Egyptians in funerary formulae, titles, etc., will become familiar to the reader. Longer inscriptions will be harder to deal with; and even experienced Egyptologists find it advisable to make transcriptions of their own that can be taken home and studied at leisure. Over the past 150 years or so, many great scholars have published their transcriptions of monumental inscriptions; but these books can usually be found only on the shelves of Egyptology libraries in universities and other specialized institutions.

The more practice a reader obtains in translating Egyptian texts, the easier it becomes to do so, and with this end in view, it would be desirable to have the means to study a varied selection of inscriptions and literary passages in printed form. Unfortunately, there is a dearth of the necessary books, although the reader may like to obtain through the

Library Service A. de Buck's 'Egyptian Reading Book' (Leyden, 1940) or A. M. Blackman's 'Middle Egyptian Stories' (Brussels, 1932) and, using these, enjoy reading various kinds of Egyptian writings in the comfort of his own home.

ABBREVIATIONS

IEH *Introducing Egyptian Hieroglyphs* (Watterson, Scottish Academic Press, 1981)

adj.	adjective
adv.	adverb
adverb.	adverbial
c.	common
cl.	clause
demonst. pro.	demonstrative pronoun
dep. pro.	dependent pronoun
f.	feminine
fem.	feminine
ff.	following
genit. adj.	genitival adjective
indep. pro.	independent pronoun
infin.	infinitive
lit.	literally
m.	masculine
masc.	masculine
n.	noun
p.	page
prep.	preposition
rel. adj.	relative adjective
rel. cl.	relative clause
sing.	singular
suffix-pro.	suffix-pronoun
var., varr.	variant(s)

Chapter 1

ADVERBS AND PREPOSITIONS

Adverbs

In Lesson 5 of IEH it was stated that there were very few true adverbs in Egyptian. The list below contains examples of (a) true adverbs and of adverbs derived from (b) prepositions (c) adjectives and (d) nouns:

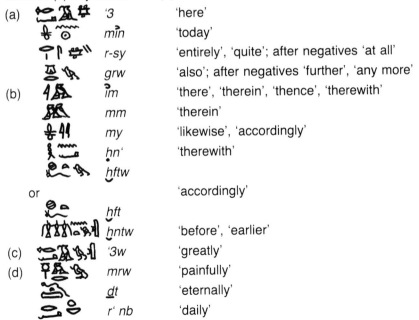

(a)		ꜥ3	'here'
		mỉn	'today'
		r-sy	'entirely', 'quite'; after negatives 'at all'
		grw	'also'; after negatives 'further', 'any more'
(b)		ỉm	'there', 'therein', 'thence', 'therewith'
		mm	'therein'
		my	'likewise', 'accordingly'
		ḥnꜥ	'therewith'
		ḫftw	
	or		'accordingly'
		ḫft	
		ḫntw	'before', 'earlier'
(c)		ꜥ3w	'greatly'
(d)		mrw	'painfully'
		ḏt	'eternally'
		rꜥ nb	'daily'

Any combination of preposition plus noun constitutes an adverbial phrase (see IEH p. 86). The following are some of the most common adverbs formed in this way:

	m-b3ḥ	'formerly'

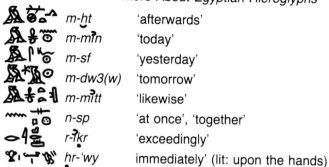

	m-ḫt	'afterwards'
	m-mỉn	'today'
	m-sf	'yesterday'
	m-dw3(w)	'tomorrow'
	m-mỉtt	'likewise'
	n-sp	'at once', 'together'
	r-ỉkr	'exceedingly'
	ḥr-ꜥwy	immediately' (lit: upon the hands)

Compound Prepositions

In Lesson 5 of IEH the reader was introduced to the more important Egyptian *simple* prepositions, that is, prepositions consisting of one word only. There is also a category of prepositions that consist of more than one word, and these are called *compound prepositions*. The compound prepositions most often used are listed below, together with their more typical meanings:

A.   Compound prepositions formed by adding a noun to one of the simple prepositions; some of these prepositions are followed by the genitival adjective ～～～ *n(y)* (see IEH p. 81) before a noun *but not* before a suffix—in the list below this type of preposition is indicated by (*n*):

1.   *n-ỉb (n)*   'for the sake (lit: heart) of'

2.   *m-ỉsw*   'in return for'

3.   *m-ꜥ*   lit: in the hand of; i.e.:

          (i) 'together with' someone (like *ḥnꜥ*)

          (ii) 'in the possession of, charge of' someone

          (iii) 'from'—e.g. receive a letter from someone, save from, inquire from

          (iv) 'through', 'because of' someone or something

4.   *m-ꜥb*   'in the company of', 'together with'

5. ᚻ𓀀 or 𓀀 *m-b3ḥ* 'in the presence of' (respected persons); lit: 'in the foreskin of'

6. ᚻᚻ *mm* 'among' people

7. ᚻ *m-h3w* (i) 'in the neighbourhood of' a person or place
    (ii) 'at the time of' someone

8. ᚻ *m-ḫ3t* 'in front of' (sometimes *m* is replaced by *r*)

9. ᚻ *r-ḫ3t* 'before' a period of time, or a person

10. ᚻ *m-h3w* 'in excess of'

11. ᚻ *ḫft-ḥr (n)* 'in front of', 'in the presence of' (lit: before the face of)

12. ᚻ *m-ḥr(y)-ỉb* 'in the midst of'

13. ᚻ *m-ḫt* 'after', 'accompanying', 'when'

14. ᚻ *m-ẖnw (n)* 'in the interior of'

15. ᚻ *m-s3* 'after' (lit: in the back of)

16. ᚻ *m-g3w* 'through lack of'

17. ᚻ *r-gs* 'at the side of', 'beside'

18. ᚻ *ḥr-tp* 'on the head of', 'on behalf of'

B. Compound prepositions formed by adding one of the simple prepositions to an adverb:

1. ᚻ *tp-m* (with suffixes *tp-ỉm*) 'before' a person or a period of time, 'in front of', 'in the direction of' a place (lit: head in)

2. ᚻ *nfryt-r* 'down to' of both place and time (lit: end to)

3. ᚻ *dr-'-r* 'right down to' (lit: end to)

4. ᚻ *wpw-ḥr* (with suffixes *wpw ḥr*) 'except', 'but' (lit: separated from)

5. ᚻ *š3'-m* 'beginning from' of place or time

C. Other compound prepositions include:

1. ᚻ *r ỉwd. . .r* 'between (one thing) and (another)'

2. ᚻ *r-ḏb3* 'instead of'

3.   〰𓏭𓊵𓏤 n-$\underline{i}kr$ (n) 'by virtue of', 'because' (lit: through the excellence of)
4.   〰𓊪𓏲𓏤 n-$mrwt$ 'in order that'

EXERCISE 1

Practise your hieroglyphic handwriting by copying out the lists of adverbs and prepositions in this Chapter. In this way you will familiarize yourself with the words and perhaps learn some of them.

Chapter 2

PARTICLES AND INTERJECTIONS

Particles

A particle is a part of speech that is neither noun, pronoun, verb, adverb nor adjective. Although in many cases particles are unimportant words characterised by the fact that they stand near or at the beginning of a sentence, occasionally particles modify that sentence in significant ways.

In Egyptian, particles are termed *enclitic* or *non-enclitic*, a description derived from the Greek word *enklitikos* 'leaning upon'. An *Enclitic particle* can never stand at the beginning of a sentence: it *must lean upon some preceding word.* A *Non-enclitic particle* can and does stand as the first word of a sentence.

A. *Non-enclitic particles*

The chief Non-enclitic particles are ⌇ *ỉn*, ⌇ *ỉḥ*, ⌇ *ỉst*, ⌇ *mk* and ⌇ *hꜣ*:

(i) ⌇ *ỉn* 'indeed' has two main uses:

    (a) to give sentences an *interrogative* force:

      e.g. ⌇

        ỉn mr.k snt.k

        do you love your sister?

    (b) to *emphasize a noun or pronoun* in the construction *ỉn* plus noun / pronoun plus the *sḏm.f* verb-form (see IEH p. 97); in this construction, the verb always has *future* sense:

e.g. 𓈖𓏏𓂋𓈖𓎡𓏤𓈖𓈖

ỉn nb ḥs.f sš

the lord, indeed, (he) will praise the scribe

It should be noted here that the pronoun employed in this construction is the Independent Pronoun (see below page 25).

N.B. The counterpart of the above construction for *past* or *present* tense employs the participles instead of the *sḏm.f* verb-form, and is dealt with on page 136.

(ii)  𓇋𓎛 ỉḥ 'then', 'therefore', 'so that' is always followed by the *sḏm.f* verb-form and expresses the *future consequence* of the action of the verb:

e.g. Open your mouth 𓇋𓎛𓏤𓂝𓎡𓈖

ỉḥ wšb.k

so that you may answer

(iii)  𓇋𓊪𓏏 ỉst, often written 𓇋𓊪𓂋 ỉst, sometimes written 𓊪𓂋 st, 𓊪𓏏 st 'lo', 'verily', etc. ỉst is often reinforced by the particles 𓂋𓆑 rf and 𓎼𓂋𓏏 grt but even when so reinforced, the particle(s) is often untranslateable; 'lo' is simply the conventional translation. ỉst has three main uses:

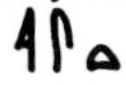

(a) to provide the necessary support for the Dependent Pronoun (see IEH page 93) in some of the constructions in which that pronoun is used (see page 44):

e.g. 𓇋𓊪𓏏𓋴𓏤𓅓𓃀𓎡𓇋

ỉst sw m b3k.ỉ

(lo) he is my servant (note the *m* of predication; cf IEH p. 106)

(b) to introduce clauses of time or circumstance:

e.g. 𓇋𓊪𓂋�𓏤𓅓𓇋𓈖𓊪𓅱

ỉst ḥm.f m ỉnpw

when His Majesty was a child (note the *m* of predication)

(c) to introduce sentences, especially when there is some expectation of further narrative:

e.g. 𓇋𓊪𓂋𓉐𓅑𓏏𓈖𓉔𓏏𓊪𓈖𓏤𓉔𓂋𓋴𓅓𓄿𓏏𓏤

ỉst rf pr Ḏḥwty-nḫt pn ḥr sm3-t3

now the house of this Djehuty-nakht was on the river bank

(iv) 𓄞𓏤 , often written 𓄞𓏤, 𓄞𓏤, 𓏤 *mk* 'behold'. The forms given above are those used when a single male person, or no one in particular, is addressed. If a single female person is addressed, the form is 𓄞𓏤 *mt* or 𓄞𓏤 *mt*; if several people are addressed, the form is 𓄞𓏤, 𓄞𓏤 *mtn* or 𓄞𓏤, 𓄞𓏤   *mtn*

e.g. 𓄞𓏤𓄿𓈖𓏤𓆓𓏤 𓂋𓈖𓇳

mk wnn rn.k r nḥḥ

Behold, your name will exist forever

𓄞𓏤𓄿𓈖𓏤 𓂋𓈖𓇳

mtn wnn rnw.tn r nḥḥ

Behold, your names will live forever

(v) 𓄿𓄿𓏤 *ḥ3*, varr. 𓄿𓏤 *ḥ3* and 𓄿𓏤 *ḥwy*, often strengthened by the particle 𓄿 *3*. The main use of *ḥ3* is to introduce a request or a wish:

e.g. 𓄿𓏤𓄿𓏤𓄿𓏤

ḥwy 3 wḏ3 ḥm.k r š n pr-'3

would Your Majesty (kindly) proceed to the lake of the Great House

B. *Enclitic particles*

The chief Enclitic particles are 𓏺 *is*, 𓂋 *rf*, 𓅓 *ḥm*, 𓋴 *swt*, 𓎼 *grt* and 𓏏𓂋 *tr*. Their position in a sentence is immediately *after* the verb (which normally comes at the beginning of a sentence; see IEH p. 101) or after the negative word, if used:

(i) 𓏺 *is* 'lo', 'indeed' has two main uses:

(a) to give emphasis or to impart a certain impressiveness to statements:

e.g. 𓄞𓏺

ḥpr.n.k is m sḏty ḥm.i

you have indeed grown up as the foster-child of My Majesty

(b) to emphasize the negative word 𓂜 *n*:

e.g. ʒc ⲓⲓ ⲁ ⲡ ⲥⲁ

n ỉs ỉr.ỉ ḫt

indeed I did not do anything

It should be noted here that even in cases where one would normally expect the negative word 〰 nn to be used (see IEH p. 105), the construction with ỉs is ʒc ⲓⲓ n ỉs, hardly ever 〰 ⲓⲓ nn ỉs:

e.g. ʒc ⲓⲓⲡ ⲯ ⲭ ⲩ ⲉ ⲥ ⲟ ⲩ

n ỉs wṯs.f dšrt

indeed he shall not wear the Red Crown

(ii) ⲉ rf (var. ⲓ ⲉ ỉrf) which can not be translated into English but indicates some kind of emphasis. It is used as follows:

(a) to indicate a wish or desire:

e.g. ⲓ ⲝ ⲑⲉ ⲥ ⲑ ⲓ ⲥ ⲓ ⲉ

sḏd.ỉ rf n.k mỉtt ỉry

let me relate to you a similar incident

(b) after plural imperatives (see below page 83)

(c) in questions:

e.g. ⲓ 〰 ⲑ ⲟ ⲑ ⲉ ⲃ ⲯ, ⲙ

ỉn nfr.ỉ rf m t3 pn

shall I be happy in this land?

(iii) ⲟ ⲃ ḥm (varr. ⲟ ⲃ ⲯ or ⲟ ⲥ) 'assuredly', 'indeed' is an Enclitic particle that lays emphasis in statements, promises and future predictions:

e.g. ⲃ ⲥ ⲃ ⲑ ⲟ ⲃ ⲯ ⲁ ⲑ

mk.ỉ ḥm s3t.ỉ

assuredly I will protect my daughter

(iv) ⲭ ⲯⲁ swt is used in statements in order to mark a contrast:

e.g. ⲥ ⲑ ⲍⲉ ⲟ ⲃ ⲥ ⲭ ⲯⲁ ⲭ

ḏd.ỉ n sḏm.n.k swt n.ỉ

I speak but you do not listen (see IEH p. 105) to me

(v) ⲥ grt is very often used to mark the beginning of a new paragraph or to reinforce descriptions. Although it can be translated as 'also', 'moreover', 'now' it is often best left untranslated:

e.g. 𓂋𓏲𓂝𓇳𓏤 𓇋𓏏𓏥𓂋𓈖𓊪𓏲𓏏 𓅓 𓋴𓈎

ʾir.ỉ grt rnpwt m ḥk3

now I spent many years as ruler

(vi) 𓂋𓏏𓂋 *tr* 'pray' is used to express surprise or indignation, and is most often found in questions:

e.g. 𓏏𓅓𓎡𓂋𓏏𓂋𓄔𓅓𓀁𓁷𓏤𓅓

tm.k tr sḏm ḥr-m

why (*ḥr-m,* see page 30) pray do you not (*tm*—negative verb, see page 141) listen

C. *Interjections*

There are very few words in Egyptian that can be classified as interjections. *ỉsṯ* 'lo' and *mk* 'behold' (see above, page 5) are the two best-known examples, whilst *hy* 'hail' also serves as an interjection:

e.g. 𓉔𓏭𓅱 𓈖𓎡

hy n.k

hail to you; or, more simply, 'hail' with 'to you' understood in English

The words 𓂝𓅱 (var. 𓂝𓏤) *ỉ* and 𓉔𓄿 *h3* are sometimes used, in religious texts especially, to introduce the *vocative*. The *vocative* is the term used for the manner in which a person is addressed. In English, this is sometimes done by prefacing a sentence with 'O' or 'Oh', e.g. 'O lord, hear my prayer'. In Egyptian, as in English, a noun in the so-called 'vocative case' is placed either at the beginning or at the end of a sentence, very seldom in the middle; and it must not interrupt the flow of a sequence of words. In Egyptian, the vocative is normally used *without* an introductory interjection:

e.g. 𓄔𓅓𓀁 𓈖𓎡 𓎟𓏭

sḏm.ỉ n.k. nb.ỉ

I am listening to you, my lord ('my lord' is in the vocative case)

When Egyptian does use an interjection to introduce the vocative, then those listed above (*ꜣ* and *hꜣ*) are used:

e.g. ![glyphs]

ꜣ nb snḏ

O lord of fear

![glyphs]

hꜣ 'nḫw

O living ones

EXERCISE 2

(a) *Write in hieroglyphs and transliteration*

1. Does he love (*sḏm.f* verb-form: see IEH p. 97) his (suffix-pronoun: see IEH p. 92) master?
2. The good servant, indeed, loves his lord exceedingly.
3. The scribe opens his mouth (for word order see IEH p. 101) so that he might answer the king.
4. Behold, I am giving bread to a hungry man daily.
5. I did indeed greet His Majesty in the presence of the entire land.
6. O my lord, assuredly I will always obey you.

(b) *Translate into English*

1. ![glyphs] (see IEH p. 82) ![glyphs]
2. ![glyphs]
3. ![glyphs] (see IEH p. 81) ![glyphs]
4. ![glyphs] (see IEH p. 105) ![glyphs]

Chapter 3

ADJECTIVES

1. *Simple adjectives*

In Lesson 4 of IEH we learned that, in Egyptian, adjectives follow the nouns that they are describing and agree with them in number and gender, the only exception being *ky* 'other'. This simple rule applies to adjectives that are being used as epithets, that is, adjectives that add something to the meaning of nouns; it needs some enlargement:

  (i) Adjectives used as epithets follow immediately after the noun they qualify and appear in the same order as they do in English:

    e.g. 𓀀𓂝𓄿𓏏𓊃𓋴𓏏𓏲

    s3t nfrt šrit

    a good little daughter

  (ii) A suffix-pronoun precedes all adjectives, remaining directly appended to its noun; and the demonstrative adjectives *pw, pn, pf* (see below p.19) take precedence over all other adjectives:

    e.g. 𓊃𓏲𓂋𓈙𓏭𓇋𓏏𓂋𓅱

    sḥrw.i ikrw

    my excellent plans

    s3.k pn nfr 𓀀𓏤𓈙𓂋𓈖𓏺𓏏𓄤

    this (demonstrative adjective) good son of yours

  (iii) If an adjective qualifies *several* nouns of *different genders,* it is normal for the adjective to be written only once (as it is in English); and for the *masculine* form to be used:

    e.g. 𓀀𓏤𓈙𓀀𓂝𓄿𓂋𓏏

    s3 s3t nb nfr

    every good son and daughter

(iv) The feminine ending ⌂ *t*, and the plural determinatives ⦙ , etc., are often omitted altogether. This is especially common with the adjective ⌣ *nb* 'every', 'any', 'all':

e.g. 𓐍𓏏 𓄤𓄤

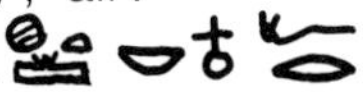

ḫt nb(t) nfr(t)

every good thing

2. Comparison of Adjectives

Adjectives can be used not only to describe a noun but also to compare one noun with another. For instance, in the sentence 'the boy is good', a simple fact is being stated: in English, the adjective 'good' is said to be in the *positive degree*. In the sentence 'the boy is better than the others', the boy is being compared with the others and the adjective 'better' is said to be in the *comparative degree*. In the sentence 'the boy is the best in his class', best (adjective) expresses an even greater degree of the boy's superiority and is said to be in the *superlative degree*.

In Egyptian, there are no special forms to indicate the degrees of comparison. Instead, the *Comparative,* as an adjective in the comparative degree is usually termed, is expressed by the preposition ⬭ *r* 'more than':

e.g. 𓉻𓂋�𓀀

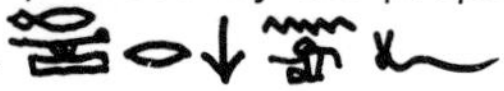

'3 r sn.f

greater than his brother

(lit: great (adjective) more than (*r*) his brother)

The *Superlative* (or adjective in the superlative degree) can be rendered in several ways:

(i) by use of the genitive, either direct or indirect:

e.g. 𓅨𓀭 𓈖 𓅨𓀭𓏥

wr n wrw

greatest of the great

(lit: great one (sing. noun) of (genitival adjective) great ones (plural noun)) nfr nfrw 🝓

the most beautiful of all

(lit: beauty (of) beauties)

(ii) by the adjective 𝄞 *ỉmy* 'who is among', 'being in', which is used as an epithet after a noun:

e.g. 🝓

wr ỉmy s'ḥw

greatest of the nobles

(lit: great one among the nobles)

(iii) by the repetition of a suffix-pronoun:

e.g. 🝓

s3.f smsw.f

his eldest son

(lit: his son his elder)

(iv) 'very' is conveyed by the adverb 🝓   *wrt* 'greatly' or by the phrase 🝓   *r ḫt nbt* 'more than anything' used to qualify an adjective:

e.g. 🝓

št3 wrt

very difficult

(lit: difficult greatly)

🝓

nfr r ḫt nbt

exceedingly beautiful

(lit: beautiful more than anything)

3. *Nisbe-adjectives*

Simple adjectives (see above page 11) can be formed from nouns and prepositions by the addition of \\ *y* as an ending or as part of an ending. The same structure is found in Semitic languages, where such adjectives are called *nisbe* or 'adjectives of relationship', and the term *nisbe* is applied to the Egyptian version also.

(i) A *nisbe*-adjective can be formed from a noun:

e.g. from the feminine noun 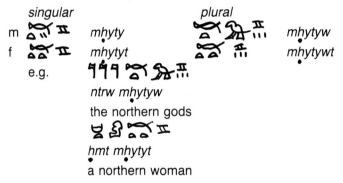 *mḥyt* 'north wind'

the *nisbe*-adjective 'northern' can be formed as follows:

singular		plural	
m	*mḥyty*		*mḥytyw*
f	*mḥytyt*		*mḥytywt*

e.g.

ntrw mḥytyw

the northern gods

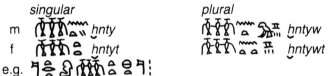

ḥmt mḥytyt

a northern woman

(ii) A *nisbe*-adjective can be formed from a preposition:

e.g. from the preposition ḫnt 'in front of', 'before' the relative *nisbe*-adjective (see page 124) can be formed as follows:

singular		plural	
m	*ḫnty*		*ḫntyw*
f	*ḫntyt*		*ḫntywt*

e.g.

ntrt ḫntyt psdt

the goddess who is at the head of the ennead

ntrwt ḫntywt r-prw.sn

the goddesses who are in front of their shrines

N.B. Where prepositions have a special form for use before suffixes (e.g. ꜣm from m; ḥr from ḥr) it is the special form that is used in the formation of the *nisbe*).

Uses of nisbe-adjectives

Nisbe-adjectives are only used as epithets (but see paragraph (iii) below) they follow the nouns they are describing and agree with them in number and gender. It should be noted however that:

(a) *nisbe*-adjectives are usually written in an abbreviated form, with *y* and *w* omitted e.g. 🐟 instead of 🐟𓈖𓈍 ; 🐟 instead of 🐟𓏏 .

(b) *nisbe*-adjectives ending in *y sound* similar to feminine duals (see IEH p. 76) and are often *written* by simply repeating an ideogram e.g. 𓏏🔘 *n̲tr ni͗wty* 'local god' (i.e. god plus the *nisbe* of the noun *ni͗wt* 'city').

The abbreviated writings, and the double ideograms, mean that *nisbe*-adjectives are often mistaken for the prepositions from which they are derived or for duals, and the beginner should bear this in mind when translating from Egyptian into English.

(iii) The *nisbe* of the genitival adjective *n(y)*.

In Middle Egyptian, the genitival adjective 〰 (see IEH p. 81) has a *nisbe* form meaning 'belong to'. It is used with *dependent pronoun* subjects only, is the only *nisbe* that *precedes* its subject, and is invariable in number and gender. The *nisbe* of the genitival adjective is most frequently used with 3rd person pronouns, and when used with them it has a special writing:

m 〰𓅱 *n-sw*; f 〰𓏏 *n-sy*

e.g. 〰𓏏 ♦🐟 ⊙ *n-sy i͗myw-ḫt Rʿ*

she belongs to the following of Re

〰 🐍 *n-wi͗ dmi͗*

I belong to the town

As far as the beginner is concerned, *nisbe*-adjectives can provide a useful supplement to vocabulary; and therefore some of the more popular *nisbes* are set out below:

🦁 (varr. 🦁, 𐤟) *i͗my-r* overseer (from *nisbe* 𓅓 derived from preposition 🦁 *m* in (form before suffix 🦁 *i͗m*)— who is in; and noun ⬭ *r* mouth, giving the literal translation 'who-is-in-the-mouth' (of subordinates). ⌐ is the hieroglyph for tongue—a pun on what is in a mouth.

ḥry-tp ʿ3 great chief

(i.e. 'he-who-is-over-the-head'—*nisbe* of preposition *ḥr* upon plus noun *tp* head plus adjective *ʿ3* great)

nṯr nỉwty local or city god

(*nisbe* of noun *nỉwt* town meaning who belongs to the town)

ḥry sšt3 he-who-is-over-the-secret (a common title—*nisbe* of preposition *ḥr* upon)

Ỉnpw tpy ḏw.f Anubis who is upon his mountain (*nisbe* of preposition *tp* upon)

sḫty peasant

(i.e. he who belongs to the country—*nisbe* of noun *sḫt* country)

ẖr(t)-nṯr necropolis

(i.e. that which is under the god—*nisbe* of preposition *ẖr*)

ḥryw-šʿ beduins

(i.e. those who are upon the sand—*nisbe* of preposition *ḥr* upon)

4. *Adjectival Expressions*

(i) 'every' is rendered by ⟨hieroglyphs⟩ *ṯnw* 'number', followed by a noun, which in turn is often followed by the adjective ⟨hieroglyph⟩ *nb* 'every', 'all', etc.:

e.g. ⟨hieroglyphs⟩

ṯnw rnpt

every year

or

𓎛𓂋𓎛𓏤𓈖𓇳𓏏𓎟

ṯnw rnpt nbt

every year

(ii) 'whole' is rendered by a noun followed by the expression 𓂋𓂧𓂋 *r-ḏr* 'to the limit' plus a suffix-pronoun which agrees with the noun:

e.g. 𓇾𓂋𓂧𓆑

t3 r-ḏr.f

the whole land (lit: the land to its limit)

(iii) 'whole' can also be rendered by a noun followed by the expression 𓏇𓇋𓂓𓆑 *mî kd.f* 'like its form', with the suffix-pronoun agreeing in number and gender with the noun:

e.g. 𓏏𓏤 𓏇𓇋𓂓𓋴𓏏

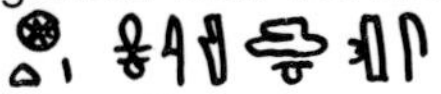

nîwt mî kd.s

the whole (or entire) town (lit: the town like its form)

(iv) 'whole', 'complete' can be rendered by a noun followed by the prepositions 𓂋 or 𓏇 , followed by 𓂋𓄿𓅱𓆑 *r (or m)-3w.f* 'according to (*r*) or like (*m*) its length' (the suffix is often omitted, but when used agrees with the noun in number and gender):

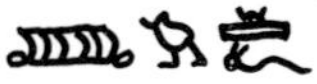

e.g. �𓇋𓂝𓇋𓏏 𓂋𓄿𓅱𓋴

ẖnyt r-3w.s

the whole crew (lit: the crew according to its length)

EXERCISE 3

(a) *Write in hieroglyphs and transliteration*

1. My local god is greater than your local god.
2. The priest goes up to the necropolis every year.
3. She gives him (see IEH p. 102) every good thing.
4. The great chief drives away the beduin who are upon this land.

(b) *Translate into English*

1. [hieroglyphs]
2. [hieroglyphs]
3. [hieroglyphs]
4. [hieroglyphs]
5. [hieroglyphs]

Chapter 4

ADJECTIVES, continued

5. *Demonstrative adjectives*

In English, demonstrative adjectives are describing words that are used to point out something; they are 'this', 'that', 'these' and 'those'.

Demonstrative adjectives are often mistaken for demonstrative pronouns (see page 32). Such confusion is avoided if it is borne in mind that adjectives must describe a noun or pronoun. If the word in question is not connected thus with a noun or pronoun, then it must be a demonstrative pronoun:

e.g. This book is yours—'this' describes the noun 'book' and is therefore a demonstrative adjective

This is your book—'this' stands alone and does not describe a noun and is therefore a demonstrative pronoun

These sweets are mine—'these' describes the noun 'sweets' and is therefore a demonstrative adjective

These are my sweets—'these' stands alone and does not describe a noun and is therefore a demonstrative pronoun

In Egyptian, the demonstrative adjectives, which like simple adjectives agree with their nouns in number and gender, are:

singular						plural		
	masculine			feminine		common		(m & f)
this	𓀀	pn	𓀀	tn	these	𓀀	nn	
this	𓀀	pw	𓀀	tw	these	𓀀	nw	
this	𓀀	p3	𓀀	t3	these	𓀀	n3	
(the)								
that	𓀀	pf	𓀀	tf	those	𓀀	nf	
	𓀀	or						
	𓀀	pfy						

(i) The plurals all *precede* their nouns and are joined to them by 〜〜 *n* (the genitival adjective). The nouns to which the plural demonstrative adjectives are appended are usually in the plural, although they are sometimes found in the singular:

e.g. 〔hieroglyphs〕

nn n sšw 'ikrw

these efficient scribes

(lit: these of scribes efficient)

〔hieroglyphs〕

nn n sḫty

these peasants

(lit: these of peasant)

(ii) *p3, t3* also precede their nouns, but are *not* joined to them by *n*:

e.g. 〔hieroglyphs〕

t3 ḥmt

this woman

(iii) The other demonstrative adjectives all *follow* their nouns; and take precedence over other adjectives:

e.g. 〔hieroglyphs〕

sḫr pn bin

this evil counsel

〔hieroglyphs〕

nṯrt tn nfrt

this good goddess

(iv) The commonest words for 'this', 'these' are *pn, tn, nn*.

(v) *pw, tw, nw* are usually found only in religious or archaic texts, or in high-flown speech:

e.g. 〔hieroglyphs〕

fnd-k pw špss

this thy noble nose

(vi) *p3, t3, n3* are the weakest of the demonstrative adjectives. They can mean 'this', 'these', and in expressions of time they are often used in preference to *pn, tn, nn*:

e.g. 𓀀𓀁𓀂𓏤𓇳

m t3 3t

at this moment

𓂝𓌅𓎬𓃒𓇳

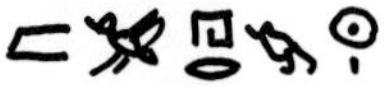

m p3 hrw

on this day *or* today

Otherwise, they are used merely as the equivalents of the definite article; and, in practice, compensate for the lack of a definite article in Middle Egyptian:

e.g. 𓀀𓈖𓏏𓇳𓀀𓌅𓀀𓂻𓊖𓉐

n3 n 't m p3 mḫr

the corn is in the storehouse

(vii) *pf, tf, nf* are often used to mean 'that' (over there) as opposed to 'this' (here):

e.g. �externally𓋴𓏛𓊪𓈖

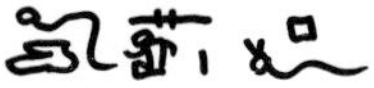

ḏd s pf

that man is speaking

However, they are sometimes used to indicate admiration, especially for things in the past; or, conversely, disgust:

e.g. 𓎼𓏤𓊖𓊪𓈖𓌢𓊪𓈖

ḫnw pf špsy

that noble Residence (i.e. palace)

but

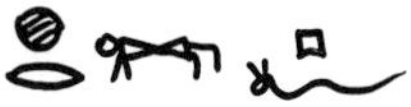

𓊖𓅓𓏛𓊪𓈖

ḫr pf

that (vile) enemy

𓈎𓀀𓅓𓏛𓊪𓈖

'wnty-sty pf

that (wretched) Nubian foreigner

(viii) The effect of the plural demonstrative adjectives preceding their nouns and being separated from them by 𓈖 *n* (see (i) above) is to turn these plurals into singular demonstrative *pronouns* rather than plural adjectives, and enables them

to stand on their own in the way that demonstrative pronouns do (see p. 32) as
the neuters 'this', 'that':

e.g. 𓆓𓂧 𓈖 𓏎𓏎

ḏd.f nn

he says this

𓂝𓏤𓏲𓏪 𓏏𓃭𓈖𓈙

pty n3

what is that? (*pty* is an interrogative pronoun—see page 29)

6. *Interrogative Adjectives*

In English, the interrogative adjectives are 'which', 'what', 'whose'. As distinct from
interrogative pronouns, which stand alone, interrogative *adjectives* must be *linked to
nouns:*

e.g. Which book do you want?—Interrogative adjective

Which is my book?—Interrogative pronoun

What road is he on?—Interrogative adjective

What is the route?—Interrogative pronoun

Whose knife is this?—Interrogative adjective

Whose is this knife?—Interrogative pronoun

In Egyptian, the interrogative adjectives 'which' and 'what' are rendered by 𓇋𓏭

varr. 𓇋𓏥 or 𓇋 *sy*, which is *invariable* in gender, and *precedes* its noun:

e.g. 𓈝𓅓𓏤𓏤 𓄇 𓇋 𓃭𓎛𓏏𓏤

šm.k ḥr s(y) w3t

on what road are you going?

(note the word order—the verb must come first in the sentence and so translated
literally the sentence reads 'you are going upon what road'?)

𓆓𓂧 𓇋𓏭 𓄙𓏏

ḏd sy ḥmt

which woman is speaking?

Egyptian has no direct equivalent of the interrogative adjective 'whose'.

Thus 'whose knife is this' would be rendered in Egyptian by the preposition 〰〰 *n*

'to' (see page 38) followed by the interrogative word 𓅓 *m*

e.g. 〰〰 𓅓 𓂞𓏤𓂺 𓈖

n m ds pn

which, translated literally, gives 'to whom (is) this knife' i.e. 'whose knife is this?'

7. *Possessive Adjectives*

see page 36

EXERCISE 4

(a) *Write in hieroglyphs and transliteration*

    1. She belongs to the master.

    2. These servants go to the town daily.

    3. The King drives out that vile foreigner from the Two Lands.

    4. Today, this girl enters into the presence of the good god.

    5. Which man says this?

(b) *Translate into English*

    1. 𓅓𓂝𓇋𓎢𓂝𓅓𓏏𓏤𓂝𓆑

    2. 𓅓𓂝𓊐𓆱𓇋𓁐𓎛𓂝𓏏𓈖

    3. 𓈖𓂋𓇋𓏤𓊖𓈖𓊪𓈖

    4. 𓄿𓅓𓀠𓇋𓂧𓅓𓄂𓄿𓏏𓆳𓊖

    5. 𓏏𓇋𓈖𓂝𓇳𓂝𓏏𓏏𓂝𓉔𓅱

Chapter 5

PRONOUNS

In Lesson 7 of IEH, it was stated that, in English, a pronoun is a word that stands in place of a noun to avoid too frequent repetition of the noun; and the Egyptian suffix- and dependent pronouns were introduced. It is time now to meet other classes of Egyptian pronoun.

In English, ten kinds of pronoun can be distinguished. They are: Personal, Indefinite, Distributive, Negative, Interrogative, Reflexive, Emphatic, Demonstrative, Possessive and Relative Pronouns. As we shall see, not all of these have strict equivalents in Egyptian.

Personal pronouns

Personal pronouns have four main purposes:
(i) to denote the person performing an action or the person who is speaking, in which instance the pronoun is said to be in the Nominative Case, and to be the subject of the sentence.

In English, personal pronouns in the Nominative Case are: I, we, you, he, she, it, they.
e.g. '*I* went to town'; '*you* told me about it'; '*she* kissed him'—the words in italic are pronouns in the Nominative Case.

In Egyptian, the personal pronouns in the Nominative Case, that is, acting as subjects of the verb and therefore of the sentence, are rendered by the suffix-pronouns (see IEH p. 93 & p. 97):

e.g. 𓂻𓏌𓏲𓈖𓊖

š*m.ỉ r nỉwt* I went to town

𓆓𓂧𓂝𓈖𓏏𓏤

ḏd.k n.ỉ ḥr.s you told me about it (lit: you spoke to me concerning it)

↓𓏏𓏛𓂋𓊃𓋴𓀁

sn.s sw she kissed him

It should be noted here that in a certain type of sentence, the subject is rendered by the independent pronoun and not by the suffix-pronoun (see below p. 45). The paradigm of the independent pronoun is set out below and should be noted for future use:

Independent pronouns

Singular				*Plural*		
𓏰	*ỉnk*	I	1st person m & f	𓏤𓊨𓈖 , 𓏤𓈖	*ỉnn*	we
			2nd person			
𓈖𓏏𓎡	*ntk*	you	m ⎱ c	𓈖𓂝𓊪𓏪	*nttn*	you
𓈖𓏏𓍿	*ntt̲*	you	f ⎰			
			3rd person			
𓈖𓏏𓆑	*ntf*	he, it	m ⎱ c	𓈖𓂝𓊪𓏪	*ntsn*	they
𓈖𓂝𓊪	*nts*	she, it	f ⎰			

(ii) to denote the direct object of an action, that is, the person or thing receiving the action of the verb, in which instance the pronoun is said to be in the Accusative Case.

In English, personal pronouns in the Accusative Case are: me, us, you, him, her, it, them.

e.g. 'he led *her* into the house'; 'the servant found *them* there'—the words in italic are pronouns in the Accusative Case.

In Egyptian, the personal pronouns in the Accusative Case, that is, acting as direct objects of the verb, are rendered by the dependent pronouns (see IEH p. 93):

e.g. 𓊪𓏭𓇓𓄿𓈗𓂻𓉐

sšm.f sy r pr he led her into the house

𓅠𓅓𓊃𓈖𓃀𓄿𓎡𓏤𓇋𓅓

gm sn b3k ỉm the servant found them there

(iii) to indicate the person or thing *to* whom or *for* whom something is done, in which instance the pronoun is said to be in the Dative Case, and is the indirect object of the verb. In English, the indirect object of the verb is often introduced by a preposition: e.g. 'he gave the bread (direct object) to me (indirect object)'. Sometimes, however, the preposition is left out: the sentence in the example quoted above could equally correctly be rendered 'he gave me the bread'—'me' is still the indirect object but without the introductory preposition.

The difficulty is compounded by the fact that in English pronouns in the Accusative Case are identical with those in the Dative Case, which are: me, us, you, him, her, it, them. A good way of testing whether or not a pronoun is in the Dative rather than the Accusative Case is to place one of the prepositions 'to' or 'for' in front of it: if the result makes sense, then the pronoun is in the Dative Case: e.g. 'he gave (to) me the bread'; 'she told (to) him her name.' We could not sensibly write 'he gave me (to) the bread' or 'she told him (to) her name'. Therefore, 'me' and not 'bread' and 'him' and not 'name' are indirect objects and are in the Dative Case; 'bread' and 'name' are direct objects and are in the Accusative Case.

N.B. The test recommended above is especially useful when translating from English into Egyptian, *when it is essential to distinguish the Dative from the Accusative.* In Egyptian, the preposition 'to' or 'for' (⌇⌇⌇ *n*) is *always* written to indicate the Dative Case, in contrast to English where, as we have seen above, 'to' is often merely understood.

As we saw in IEH, Lesson 7, the suffix-pronouns are used after prepositions. The construction, therefore, of the Dative Case of the personal pronoun in Egyptian is the preposition ⌇⌇⌇ *n* (the datival *n*) plus the relevant suffix-pronoun:

e.g.

dỉ.f n.ỉ t

he gave me the bread (lit: he gave to me bread)

ḏd.s n.f rn.s

she told him her name (lit: she said to him her name)

(iv) to indicate possession: the pronoun that indicates ownership is said to be in the

Genitive or Possessive Case. In English, the personal pronouns in the Possessive Case are: mine, ours, yours, his, hers, its, theirs.

Although both independent and suffix-pronouns are used to indicate possession (see below p.36), strictly speaking there is no equivalent in Egyptian of English personal pronouns in the Possessive Case.

Indefinite pronouns

In English, the indefinite pronouns are those that are not specific about the person or thing referred to: for example, some, somebody, few, any, one, another, etc.:

e.g. '*some* went, *few* stayed'; 'Sir, I have not *any*'; '*somebody* knocked at the door'; '*one* ran, *another* walked'.

In Egyptian, there is only one true indefinite pronoun— ⌂𓏏 *tw* 'one':

e.g. 𓆓𓂧 ⌂𓏏

　　ḏd tw one says

Instead, Egyptian tends to use nouns, sometimes combined with adjectives in short phrases, which represent what are, in English, indefinite pronouns:

(i) Somebody, anyone, any (when it really means any man, any men) some (when it really means some men) are represented in Egyptian by the noun 𓊃𓏤 *s* man:

　　e.g. 𓄿𓀁𓄣𓊃𓏤

　　sḏm.ỉ s I heard somebody

　　𓈖 𓄿𓀁𓄣𓊃𓏤

　　n sḏm.ỉ s I did not hear anyone

　　𓊃𓏤 𓏏𓂋 𓈙𓊃𓂻

　　s ḥr šs some were running (for the construction *ḥr šs* see page 90)

(ii) Something, any (when it really means any thing) are represented in Egyptian by the noun 𓐍𓏏 *ḥt* things:

　　e.g. 𓂋𓂝 𓈖𓊃𓈖 𓐍𓏏

　　rdỉ.f n.sn ḥt he is giving something to them

　　𓈖𓈖 𓂋𓂝 𓈖𓐍𓏏

　　nn rdỉ.f (see IEH p. 105) *n.ỉ ḥt* he will not give me any (or anything)

(iii) Few is rendered by the noun 𓏏𓏤 *nhy* a little, plus indirect genitive (see IEH p. 81) plus noun in the singular:

e.g.

nhy n rmt few (lit: few of people)

nhy n niwt few cities

(iv) One, other, another are rendered by combinations of *wʿ* one (m), *wʿt* one (f), *sn-nw.f* his second and *ky* other (m) or *kt* other (f):

e.g.

wʿ m niwt ky m sht

one was in the town, the other was in the country

or

one was in the town, another was in the country

wʿ dd.f hft sn-nw.f

one said to the other (lit: one he said before his fellow)

wʿt dd.s hft sn-nw.s one (woman) said to another

hpt kt kt one (woman) embraced the other

It will be noted that in many of the examples quoted above, the indefinite pronoun could equally well have been translated literally as a noun: e.g. 'I heard somebody' could have been translated as 'I heard a/the man'; 'one was in the town' as 'one man was in the town', etc. It is often left to the translator to judge on context which translation to use.

Distributive pronouns

In English, the distributive pronouns are: each, everyone, either, neither, etc.

e.g. *everyone* would like a little of *each; either* would suffice, or *neither.*

In Egyptian, the distributive pronouns either, neither are not expressed in a concrete way;

they are sometimes supplied in his English version by the translator if the context seems to demand it.

Each, everyone, etc., are rendered in Egyptian by a combination of nouns and adjectives:

(i) 𓊃𓏤𓏏 𓎟 *s nb* (lit: every man) is the most common expression for everyone, everybody; it is also used to represent each one, each.

(ii) 𓃀𓅱𓊌 *bw nb* (lit: every place) is also commonly found as the distributive pronoun everyone.

(iii) 𓁷𓏤 𓎟 *ḥr nb* (lit: every face) is found frequently as the distributive pronoun everyone.

(iv) 𓁹𓏤 𓎟 *wʿ nb* (every one) can be translated as each one.

(v) 𓐍𓏏𓏤 𓎟𓏏 *ḫt nbt* (lit: all things) is used with the meaning everything.

e.g.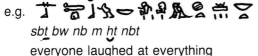

sbṯ bw nb m ḫt nbt

everyone laughed at everything

Negative pronouns

In English, the negative pronouns are none, no one e.g. 'none shall sleep'.

In Egyptian, none, no one, is expressed by the noun 𓊃𓏤 *s* man plus a negative word:

e.g. 𓂜𓈖 𓅱𓈖 𓄣 𓈖 𓊃𓏤

nn wn (see below p.39) *ỉb n s* (see also p. 38) no one has a heart (lit: not is a heart to a man)

Interrogative pronouns

In English, the interrogative pronouns are: who? what? which? and they are used to ask questions e.g. who did it? what is his name? which is the winner?

In Egyptian, there are four main interrogative pronouns:

(i)   〔glyph〕 (also written 〔glyph〕 or 〔glyph〕) *m* is the most common word for *who?*
what? It usually stands at the beginning of the sentence, very often preceded by the
particle 〔glyph〕 *ỉn* (see p. 5) for emphasis:

e.g. 〔glyph〕

ỉn m ỉr st who made it?

N.B. The combination of *ỉn* with *m* is sometimes shortened to 〔glyph〕 *n-m*:

e.g. 〔glyph〕 *n-m ỉn tw* who has brought you?

〔glyph〕 is sometimes combined with a preposition. As we saw in Lesson 5 of IEH,
a preposition plus a noun forms an adverbial phrase. Just so does a preposition plus
the pronoun 〔glyph〕 form an adverbial phrase.

For instance, the preposition 〔glyph〕 *mỉ* like prefaced to 〔glyph〕 *m* means, literally,
like what? Similarly, *m* prefaced by the preposition 〔glyph〕 *ḥr* on account of is translated,
literally, *as on account of what?* Less literally, 〔glyph〕 *mỉ m* can be translated as
how? and 〔glyph〕 *ḥr m* as *why?*

When *m* is used with a preposition, it follows the normal rules of word order (see
p. 131) which in this instance decree that *mỉ* or *ḥr m*, being adverbial phrases, should
come last in a sentence:

e.g. 〔glyph〕

wnn t3 pf mỉ m

how shall that (*pf*) land fare?

〔glyph〕

tm.t ḥn ḥr m

why do you not (*tm.t*: see below p. 143) row (*ḥn*)

(ii)   〔glyph〕 *ptr* means *who? what? which?*; it can be written 〔glyph〕 *pty*; and it
stands at the beginning of the sentence:

e.g. 〔glyph〕

ptr rn.k what is your name?

〔glyph〕

pty sy which is it?

(iii) 〔glyph〕 *ỉšst* means *what?* and obeys the normal rules of word order in sentences:

e.g. 𓄿𓈖𓏤𓏏𓂝𓊪

ỉr.k n.f ỉšst

what are you doing to him?

(i.e. verb, dative plus suffix-pronoun, interrogative pronoun)

(iv) 𓅲𓏭 (or 𓅲 , 𓅲𓏏) *sy* means who? what? It is rarely used except in Non-verbal Sentences (see below page 42):

e.g. 𓅲𓏭𓊪𓊹𓈖𓈖

sy pw nṯr pn

who is (see p. 43 for *pw* meaning 'is') this god?

Reflexive pronouns

In English, the reflexive pronouns are: myself, yourself, himself, herself, itself, ourselves, yourselves, themselves. They indicate that the action of the verb turns back upon the subject, that the subject is performing the action upon himself: e.g. she sat herself down; he placed himself on the mat; I asked myself if I could do it. In Egyptian, there are no special reflexive pronouns. Instead, both (i) suffix and (ii) dependent pronouns can be used reflexively:

e.g. (i) 𓆓𓂧𓈖

ḏd.f n.f can be translated 'he said to him' with 'him' meaning a different person from the subject of the verb, 'he'.

However, the second suffix-pronoun *f* could equally well be translated as a reflexive pronoun, thus giving 'he said to himself'.

(ii) 𓂋𓂧𓂋𓏤𓄿𓂋

rdỉ.f sw ḥr ẖt-f

he placed himself on his belly, where the dependent pronoun *sw* is used reflexively.

Emphatic pronouns

In English, the emphatic pronouns are the same as the reflexive pronouns (myself, yourself, etc). They can be distinguished from the reflexive pronouns in use in that they pick up the subject of the sentence in order to emphasize it: e.g. I myself will go; she herself sat down; I myself asked if I could do it. Compare, and note the difference, between the last two examples and examples one and three in the first paragraph of the section on reflexive pronouns.

In Egyptian, there are no special emphatic pronouns. Instead, use is made of 𓂧𓋴 *ds* plus a suffix-pronoun. The construction is subject plus *ds* plus suffix-pronoun, with the suffix agreeing in number and gender with the subject:

e.g. 𓆓𓂧𓂧𓂧𓋴

ḏd.í ḏs.í I myself said

𓇳𓂧𓋴𓆑

R' ḏs.f Re himself

𓉐𓃀𓈖𓂧𓋴𓆑𓏤𓏏𓏛

ḥ3b nb ḏs.f sš the master himself sent the scribe

Demonstrative pronouns

Demonstrative pronouns are those that point out or identify a person or an object. In English, they are: this, that, these, those, such, same.

As with the possessive pronouns, care must be taken to distinguish between a demonstrative pronoun and a demonstrative adjective:

e.g. 'this house is mine'—'this' qualifies 'house' and is therefore a demonstrative *adjective*

'this is my house'—'this' stands alone, does not describe a noun (or pronoun) and is

therefore a demonstrative *pronoun*.

In Egyptian, the demonstrative pronouns are often identical with certain demonstrative adjectives, which means that especial care must be taken to distinguish between them. The demonstrative pronouns are:

(i) 𓈖𓈖 *nn* (var. 𓈖𓈖𓈖) this. 𓈖𓈖 *nn* is the plural of the demonstrative adjective 𓊪𓈖 *pn* (see page 19); but it can be treated as singular and used as a demonstrative pronoun meaning 'this':

e.g. 𓆓𓂝𓏤

    <u>d</u>d. f nn he said this

(ii)   𓈖𓏤 n3 is the plural of 𓊪𓏤 p3, which is most often used as a demonstrative adjective but can be used as the definite article (see page 21).   𓈖𓏤 n3, like nn, can be treated as singular and used as a demonstrative pronoun meaning 'this':

e.g. 𓊪𓏏𓂋 𓈖𓏤

    ptr n3 what is this?

(iii) 𓊪𓏤 p3, besides being a demonstrative adjective (see page 19), is also used as the demonstrative pronoun meaning 'such':

e.g. 𓊪𓏤𓅱𓊨𓁹

    p3 pw ws*i̭r* such is (pw) Osiris

(iv) 𓊪𓆑𓏤 pf3 means 'that' (see below)

(v) 𓈖 pn is normally found as a demonstrative adjective (see page 19), but is occasionally found as the demonstrative pronoun 'this':

e.g. 𓂋𓐍𓇋𓊪𓆑𓏤𓂋𓈖

    r<u>h</u>.*i̭* pf3 r pn

    I know that from this

Possessive pronouns

Possessive pronouns denote possession or ownership. In English, they are identical with the personal pronouns in the genitive case (see page 27) and are: mine, yours, his, hers, its, theirs.

    Possessive pronouns must not be confused with possessive adjectives: possessive adjectives qualify a noun; possessive pronouns stand alone in the sentence:

e.g.	this gold	is his
	(demonstrative adjective + noun)	(possessive pronoun)
	this	is his gold
	(demonstrative pronoun)	(possessive adjective + noun)

In Egyptian, there are no strict equivalents of the English possessive pronouns mine, yours, etc. Instead of saying the Egyptian version of 'is his' ('his' being a possessive pronoun in English), Egyptian says the equivalent of 'belongs to him' using the independent pronoun (see page 38):

e.g. *the gold is his* is rendered in Egyptian by the independent pronoun (3rd person masc.) followed by the noun, gold, as subject:

ntf nbw

lit: him gold, understood to be *to* him *belongs* (the) gold

i.e. the gold is his

she is mine is rendered in Egyptian by the independent pronoun (3rd person fem.) followed by the pronoun, mine, as subject (N.B. the pronoun subject here is expressed by a dependent pronoun):

ỉnk sy

lit: me she, understood to be *to* me *belongs* she

i.e. she is mine

this house is theirs is rendered in Egyptian by the independent pronoun (3rd person plural) followed by the noun, house, qualified by the demonstrative adjective, this, as subject:

ntsn pr pn

lit: theirs house this, understood to be *to* them *belongs* this house

i.e. this house is theirs.

Relative pronouns

Relative pronouns serve as conjunctions to join together two sentences. In English, the relative pronouns are who, which, whoever, whom, whose.

e.g. 'this is the man *who* did it'; 'this is the man *whom* I saw'; 'this is the man to *whom* I
   gave the book'; 'this is the bread *which* was given to me'.
The relative pronouns above are really acting as *adjectives*, since they introduce groups
of words that describe the subject of the sentence (i.e. man, bread).
   In Egyptian, there are no relative pronouns. Instead, Egyptian has a relative adjective
(see below, page 120).

EXERCISE 5

(a) *Write in hieroglyphs and transliteration*
   1. A few go into the town every day.
   2. Everyone is giving him something.
   3. One was in the temple and the other was in his house.
   4. What is she doing?
   5. You yourself said this.

(b) *Translate into English*
   1. ⲟ⳨⳨⳨
   2. ⳨⳨⳨
   3. ⳨⳨⳨
   4. ⳨⳨⳨
   5. ⳨⳨⳨

Chapter 6

POSSESSION

A. *Ownership of an object*

In English, the simplest way of expressing ownership or possession of something is to use the *possessive adjectives* my, your, his, her, its, our, their: e.g. my house, her book, their sister. It has already been noted (see page 33) that, since adjectives are 'describing words', they must qualify a noun; and the distinction has been drawn between a possessive pronoun and a possessive adjective:

e.g. 'this house is mine'—'mine' is a possessive pronoun (see page 33)

'this is my house'—'my' is a possessive adjective.

In Egyptian, the suffix-*pronouns* can be used to denote possession (see IEH, p. 93):

e.g.　🏠𓎡 *pr.i* my house　↓〰𓂸𓏭𓏥 *snt.sn* their sister

When the suffix-pronouns are used to indicate possession, they are in fact being added on to nouns as *direct genitives* (see IEH, p. 80). Thus, strictly speaking, *pr.i* (above) is noun plus direct genitive (i.e. not expressed) plus suffix-pronoun, and really means 'house of me' (= my house); similarly, *snt.sn* (above) means 'sister of them' (= their sister). It is standard practice, however, to translate noun plus suffix-pronoun as though the pronoun were a possessive adjective.

Occasionally, however, a true possessive adjective was used in Middle Egyptian, the paradigm of which is set out below. The Egyptian possessive adjective is, in effect, the suffix-pronouns prefaced by (i) 𓊪𓏭𓏭 *p3y* when used with masculine nouns, (ii) 𓆳𓏏𓏭𓏭 *t3y* when used with feminine nouns and (iii) 𓈖𓏭𓏭 *n3y* when used with plural nouns of either gender.

The Possessive Adjective
with singular masculine nouns

　　𓊪𓏭𓏭𓎡　*p3y.i*　1st sing., c.　my

𓊪𓏭𓎡	p3y.k	2nd sing., c.	your
𓊪𓏭𓆑	p3y.f	3rd sing., m.	his, its
𓊪𓏭𓋴	p3y.s	3rd sing. f.	her, its
𓊪𓏭𓈖	p3y.n	1st plural, c.	our
𓊪𓏭𓏏𓈖	p3y.$\underline{t}$n	2nd plural, c.	your
𓊪𓏭𓋴𓈖	p3y.sn	3rd plural c.	their

with singular feminine (or neuter) nouns

𓏏𓏭𓇋	t3y.$\overset{?}{i}$	1st sing., c.	my
𓏏𓏭𓎡	t3y.k	2nd sing., c.	your

etc.

with plural nouns

𓈖𓏭𓇋𓈖	n3y.$\overset{?}{i}$ n	1st sing., c.	my
𓈖𓏭𓎡𓈖	n3y.k n	2nd sing., c.	your

etc.

Note 1

The possessive adjective is written *before* its noun; the *singular* possessive adjective is directly appended to the following noun, but the *plural* possessive adjective is joined to its noun by 𓈖 *n*.

Note 2

The *prefix* of the possessive adjective (𓊪𓏭 , 𓏏𓏭 , 𓈖𓏭) agrees with its noun in number and gender; the *suffix-pronoun element* of the possessive adjective agrees with the person who 'owns' the noun:

e.g.	her house	p3y.s pr
	my house	p3y.$\overset{?}{i}$ pr
	his wife	t3y.f ḥmt
	your wife	t3y.k ḥmt
	her children	n3y.s n ẖrdw
	their wives	n3y.sn n ḥmwt

B. *Sentences expressing possession*
Egyptian *has no verbs meaning* 'possess', 'own', 'have', 'belong to'. Therefore, since a sentence must have a verb in it, strictly speaking there are no *sentences* expressing possession in Egyptian. However, the Egyptians had several constructions by which they conveyed the meaning of the English verbs 'possess', 'own', etc.

1. The preposition 〰〰 *n* 'to'

In this construction, the noun denoting the object possessed is followed by 〰〰 *n*, followed by the noun or suffix-pronoun denoting the possessor of the object:

e.g. [hieroglyphs]

ḫt n sn.ỉ

The literal translation of the above is:

property (*ḫt*) is (not expressed: see below p. 41) to (*n*) my brother (*sn.ỉ*) i.e. the property belongs to my brother

N.B. When 〰〰 *n* is followed by a suffix-pronoun, they must take precedence over other pronouns and nouns in the sentence:

e.g. [hieroglyphs]

n.k st it belongs to you (lit: to (*n*) you (*.k*—suffix-pronoun) it (dependent pronoun)

[hieroglyphs]

ỉw (see below p. 48) *n.ỉ ḫt.ỉ nbt* all my property belongs to me

2. If the possessor is denoted by a *pronoun* rather than a noun; and if it is desired to place some emphasis on the possessor, then one of the following constructions may be used:

(a) an independent pronoun followed by a noun or *dependent* pronoun, which can be translated as 'I am (you are, he is etc.) the owner of X'; or 'to me (to you, to him etc.) belongs X':

e.g. [hieroglyphs] *ntk nbw* you are the owner of the gold

[hieroglyphs] *ỉnk sy* she belongs to me

[hieroglyphs] *ntf snṯr* to him belongs the incense

(this example could, if the context so demands,

be translated with less emphasis on the possessor, as 'the incense belongs to him').

(b) 〰 *n* plus an appropriate *suffix*-pronoun plus ⸢𓇋𓐠⸣ *ỉmy* (probably derived
from the adverb 𓇋𓅓 *ỉm* 'there'):

e.g. 𓂝𓇋𓐠𓏏𓏤

   n.k-ỉmy nbw   to you belongs the gold

                                   or

                                   the gold belongs to you

   𓂝𓇋𓇋𓇋𓐠𓉐

   n.sn-ỉmy prw   to them belong the houses

                                   or

                                   the houses belong to them

3. The notion of I have (you have, he has etc.), or I had, X, is conveyed by the verb
   𓂝𓏤 *wnn* 'exist', often preceded by one of the particles 𓇋𓅱 *ỉw* or 𓇋𓊃 (or

   𓂝) *ỉsṯ*:

e.g. 𓇋𓊃𓂝𓏤𓅱𓂝𓏤

   ỉst wn ḥmt.f and he has (or had) a wife

                 lit: lo, exists (the) wife (of) him

4. The noun 𓎟 *nb* 'lord' can be used to express possession, in which case it is
   usually followed by a direct genitive, i.e. a noun/pronoun that is *not* preceded by
   the genitival adjective 〰 *n* (see IEH, p. 80); *nb* is preceded by the appropriate
   independent pronoun:

e.g. 𓄿𓎟𓂝𓃭

   ỉnk nb ʿꜣw

   I own the donkeys (lit: I am the lord/owner of donkeys)

   𓈖𓏏𓎟𓏏𓎳

   nts nbt ḥḏ

   she owned the silver

C. To convey the notion of *not* owning something, or *not to have* something, the negative word 〰 *nn* is used:

e.g. 〰 〰 𓊪𓂝

    nn n.f st it does not belong to him

        (lit: not to him it)

〰 𓅓 𓏤 〰 𓀀

nn wn ỉb n s no man has a heart

        (lit: not exists a heart to a man)

〰 𓅓 𓁶

nn wn tp.f he has no head

        (lit: not exists a head of him)

EXERCISE 6

(a) *Write in hieroglyphs and transliteration*

    1. All lands belong to him, to him belongs heaven.

    2. You are the ruler of eternity and lord of everlasting.

    3. These asses belong to my brother.

    4. One of the men has no beard.

    5. He has no water.

(b) *Translate into English*

    1.
    2.
    3.
    4.
    5.

Chapter 7

NON-VERBAL SENTENCES

In English, a sentence is a group of words in which the vital part is a verb; without a verb, the group of words is merely a phrase. Sentences are divided into two parts: subject and predicate, the subject being what is spoken about, the predicate being what is said about the subject:

e.g.

subject	predicate
Birds	fly in the sky
The sun	is in the sky

In Egyptian, as we learned in IEH (p. 106), there is no verb 'to be', and a sentence such as 'the sun is in the sky' is formed by placing the subject (sun) in direct juxtaposition to the predicate (in the sky). Sentences that in English employ the verb 'to be' are, in Egyptian, composed according to what is being said about the subject of the sentence: is the subject being enlarged by a noun, an adverb, an adjective (or their equivalents)? e.g. I am a man: in this example, the subject 'I' is amplified by the noun 'man'.

I am here: 'I' is amplified by the adverb 'here'.

I am happy: 'I' is amplified by the adjective 'happy'. *In English*, 'I am happy' is rendered by using the adjective 'happy' plus the verb 'to be' in the capacity of an auxiliary or helping verb. *In Egyptian*, there is the possibility of rendering what in English is an adjective plus the verb 'to be' by a so-called adjective-verb (see below p. 46).

It should be borne in mind that in Egyptian *it is not the verb 'to be' that is important* as much as whether the predicate (what is said about the subject) is a noun, an adverb or an adjective.

A sentence that in English employs the verb 'to be' but that in Egyptian is without it is called *a non-verbal sentence.* Such sentences either express identity, state a simple fact or pose a simple question. They can be translated into past, present or future tense according to context, and consist of two essential elements, subject and predicate.

The *subject* of a non-verbal sentence may be: (i) a noun (ii) a suffix-pronoun (iii) a dependent pronoun (iv) an independent pronoun or (v) a demonstrative pronoun.

N.B. on (ii) a suffix-pronoun, by its very nature, must be used with an introductory word, normally 𓇋𓅱 *iw*, 𓃹𓈖 *wnn* or 𓃹𓈖 *wn*, supplied in non-verbal sentences for suffix-pronouns to 'lean on'.

(iii) a dependent pronoun can be used only after a) a particle such as 𓅓𓂝 *mk* behold (see page 5) or b) the negative 𓂜 *nn* or c) an adjective.

(iv) an independent pronoun *cannot be used if the predicate is an adverb.*

The *predicate* of a non-verbal sentence may be: i) a noun ii) an adjective iii) an adverb iv) an adverbial phrase (i.e. a preposition plus a noun). *Non-verbal sentences are classified according to what their predicates consist of:*

e.g. *Subject   Predicate*

The man	is a king	'king' is a noun: the sentence, therefore, is one with *nominal predicate*
The man	is good	'good' is an adjective: the sentence, therefore, is one with *adjectival predicate*
The man	is there	'there is an adverb: the sentence, therefore, is one with *adverbial predicate*
The man	is in the town	'in the town' is an adverbial phrase consisting of a preposition (in) and a noun (town): the sentence, therefore, is one with *adverbial predicate*

Non-verbal sentences with nominal predicate

A. *with a noun as subject*

1. Where *both* subject *and* predicate are *nouns,* direct juxtaposition may be used, with subject *preceding* predicate:

e.g. 𓀀𓏤𓇓𓈖𓀝 *s nsw* the man is a king

N.B. The *predicate* precedes the *subject* if (i) the subject is an interrogative pronoun or (ii) 𓂋𓈖𓆑 *rn.f* (or *rn.s*) his (or her) name:

e.g. 𓊪𓇋𓂋𓀀 𓇓 *pir s* who is the man?

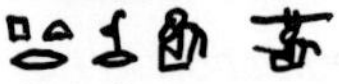

� 𓂋𓈖𓆑 *ddỉ rn.f* his name is Djedi

2. The use of direct juxtaposition became obsolete in Middle Egyptian. Instead, the predicate tended to be introduced by the *m* of predication (see IEH, p. 106), turning what looks like a nominal predicate in English into an adverbial predicate in Egyptian (see below p. 47):

e.g. 𓇓𓂝𓏤𓇋𓈖𓀝

s m nsw the man is a king

(lit: the man is as/in the position of a king)

3. Once the direct juxtaposition method became obsolete, a construction using the demonstrative pronoun 𓊪𓅱 *pw* (var. 𓊪) became popular. In this construction, *pw* was no longer used as a demonstrative pronoun with the meaning 'this', 'that', but instead had the meaning of the third person pronouns 'he', 'she', 'it' or 'they'. When *pw* is used, the word order is predicate, *pw*, subject, with *pw* being invariable no matter what gender or number the subject is. This type of sentence is often called a B *pw* A sentence, B being the predicate, A being the subject:

e.g. 𓇋𓈖𓀝𓊪𓅱𓇓 *nsw pw s*

the man is a king

(lit: king this man)

N.B. *pw* normally follows immediately after the predicate. But if the predicate consists of several words, or contains an indirect genitive, *pw* is often inserted after the *first* word, leaving the rest to come after:

e.g. 𓏏𓄿𓊪𓅱𓄤𓇋𓄿𓄿𓂋𓈖𓆑

t3 pw nfr ỉ33 rn.f

it was a good land whose name was Yaa

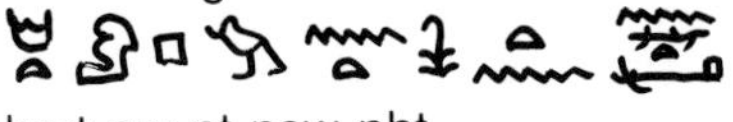

𓈞𓏏𓊪𓅱𓈖𓏏𓇓𓈖𓐍𓏏

hmt pw nt nsw nḫt

she is the wife of a mighty king

B. *with a pronoun as subject*

1. If the *subject* of a sentence with nominal predicate is a *first* or *second person pronoun*, singular or plural (i.e. I, we, you), then the independent pronouns are used, with subject and predicate juxtaposed; the *m of predication is not used:*

   e.g. ꜣnk nb.k I am your lord

   ntk s you are a man

   nttn sšw you are scribes

2. If the subject is *third person*, singular or plural (i.e. he, she, it, they), the above construction is *not* normally used. Instead, there is a choice of methods:

   (i) 3rd person suffix-pronoun, introduced by ꜣw, wn, etc., *plus m of predication:*

   e.g. ꜣw.s m ẖrd she is a child (see also para. ii below)

   or

   3rd person dependent pronoun, introduced by a particle such as mk, plus *m* of predication:

   e.g. mk sy m ẖrd (behold) she is a child

   (ii) a demonstrative pronoun such as nn 'this', 'these' or pw (see above). In such cases, the word order is predicate followed by demonstrative pronoun subject:

   e.g. dpt mt nn this is the taste of death

   dpt mt pw it is the taste of death

   ẖrd pw she is a child

   Note that *pw* is used whether the subject is masculine, feminine, singular or plural.

C. *with a pronoun as predicate*

   The predicate in non-verbal sentences with nominal predicate can be a *pronoun* rather than a noun e.g. 'It is I'. In such cases, the pronoun used is the independent pronoun; the subject is rendered by *pw*; and the word order is predicate followed by *pw*:

e.g.   𓏏𓃒𓊡 *ỉnk pw* it is I

        𓈖𓏏𓆑 𓊡 *ntf pw* it is he

Negation

Non-verbal sentences with nominal predicate are usually negated by placing the negative word 𓂜 *nn* at the beginning of the sentence:

e.g. 𓂜 𓏏𓃒𓀀 *nn ỉnk s* I am not a man

      𓂜 𓈖𓏏𓆑 𓊡 *nn ntf pw* it is not he

However, ⌒ *n* or ⌒   𓈖𓏏 *n .... ỉs* is sometimes found:

e.g. ⌒ 𓏏𓃒𓎟𓎡 *n ỉnk nb.k* I am not your lord

      ⌒ 𓈖𓏏𓎡 𓀀 *n ntk ỉs s* you are not a man

Non-verbal sentences with adjectival predicate

A. *with a noun as subject*

In the sentence 'the man is good', 'man', the subject, is a noun; 'good' is an adjective in that it describes the noun. In Egyptian, the adjectival predicate, 'good' is placed in direct juxtaposition *before* the noun subject 'man', giving

            𓄤 𓀀 *nfr s*

            the man is good (lit: good the man)

B. *with a pronoun as subject*

1. When the subject is the 1st person (I, we), the independent pronoun is used. The order is: subject, predicate; and if the the subject is feminine, the predicate is usually made to agree:

   e.g. 𓏏𓃒𓄤 *ỉnk nfr* I (m.) am good

         𓏏𓃒𓄤𓏏 *ỉnk nfrt* I (f.) am good

2. When the subject is the 2nd or 3rd person (you, he, she, it, they), the dependent pronouns are used. The order is: predicate, subject, with the predicate being invariable no matter what the number or gender of the subject is:

e.g.   𓄤 *nfr sw* he is good

         𓄤 *nfr st* she is good

N.B. The ending 𓀡" *-wy* is sometimes added to adjectival predicates in order to give them exclamatory force:

e.g.   𓄤 *nfr-wy pr pn* how beautiful is this house!

C. Most Egyptian adjectives, with the exception of *nisbe*-adjectives (see page 13), have a corresponding verb-form. Thus, for example, 𓄤 *nfr* can be an adjective meaning 'good' and also a verb (called *an adjective-verb*) meaning 'be good'. Thus it is impossible to say whether the construction adjectival predicate plus *noun* subject is a non-verbal sentence or one employing the *sḏm.f*-form of an adjective verb; the word order is the same for both, and the adjective/adjective-verb has no distinguishing marks.

    The position is more clear when the subject is a pronoun: the adjectival predicate *must* employ a dependent pronoun whereas the adjective-verb must employ a suffix-pronoun:

e.g.   𓄤 *nfr tw ḥnꜥ.ỉ* you are happy with me

                                        (adj. pred. + dep. pro.)

        𓄤 *nfr.k ḥnꜥ.ỉ* you are happy with me

                                          (adj.-verb + suffix-pro.)

When translating from English into Egyptian, the choice between these two constructions is usually a matter of personal preference. There are occasions, however, on which the construction adjectival predicate, subject, *must* be rendered by employing the *sḏm.f*-form of the adjective verb:

(i) in clauses of purpose:

    e.g. I have given this to you

       wr.k ỉm.s k3.k ỉm.s ꜥ3.k ỉm.s so that you may be great by

means of it, so that you may be exalted by means of it, so that you may be eminent by means of it

(ii) after the verb *rdỉ* 'cause' (see page 75):

e.g.

dỉ.ỉ wr rn.k

I will cause your name to be great

dỉ.ỉ wr.f

I will cause him to be great

Negation

(a) If the subject of a non-verbal sentence with adjectival predicate is a *pronoun*, the sentence is negated by means of ⌇ *n* placed at the beginning of the sentence:

e.g.   *n ỉnk nfr* I am not good

   n nfr st she is not good

(b) If the subject of a non-verbal sentence with adjectival predicate is a *noun*, the sentence is negated by either ⌇ *n* or ⌇ *nn* placed before the predicate (which is, of course, placed before the subject).

In this case, the predicate should be regarded as an *adjective-verb*; and just as *nn sḏm.f* indicates future tense and *n sḏm.f* indicates past (see IEH p. 105), so *nn* placed before an adjectival predicate usually gives a notion of futurity and *n* plus adjectival predicate can often be translated as past tense:

e.g.   *nn wr s* the man will not be great

   n nfr s the man was not good

Non-verbal sentences with adverbial predicate

Sentences with adverbial predicate are those in which the predicate consists of a true adverb, or an adverbial phrase (preposition plus noun). The preposition is often the *m* of predication; the ⌇ *n* of possession (see page 38); or ⬭ *r*, the preposition which indicates futurity, although other prepositions are used. The subject may be a noun or a pronoun.

The word order in sentences with adverbial predicate is: subject (noun or pronoun), predicate (adverb or adverbial phrase).

1. *Noun subject*

    e.g. the man is there 𓀀𓏤 𓇋𓐠 *s ỉm*

        the man is in the town 𓀀𓏤 𓐠𓊖 *s m nỉwt*

    N.B. If a non-verbal sentence with adverbial predicate is introduced as follows: 𓇋𓅱 *ỉw* followed by *noun* subject, the sentence should be regarded as having some importance. *ỉw* does not normally introduce subordinate clauses (but see below).

2. *Pronoun subject*

    If the subject of the sentence is a pronoun, the *suffix*-pronouns are normally used. However, a suffix-pronoun cannot stand alone, it must be preceded by some supporting word—in this case, 𓇋𓅱 *ỉw*:

    e.g. he is there   𓇋𓅱𓆑 𓇋𓐠 *ỉw.f ỉm*

        he is in the town   𓇋𓅱𓆑 𓐠𓊖 *ỉw.f m nỉwt*

The use of *ỉw* in this instance, therefore, does *not* indicate that the sentence should be translated as a main clause. The examples cited above could equally well have been translated as subordinate clauses: 'when he is there'; 'although he was in the town', etc. In these instances, *ỉw* is merely being used as the support for a suffix-pronoun.

Negation

 (i) *nominal subject without ỉw*

    𓂜 *nn* is used, and is placed before the subject:

    e.g.   𓂜 𓀀𓏤 𓇋𓐠 *nn s ỉm* the man is not there

 (ii) *nominal subject with ỉw*

    𓂜 *nn* is used, and is placed *between ỉw* and the subject:

    e.g.   𓇋𓅱 𓂜 𓀀𓏤 𓇋𓐠 *ỉw nn s ỉm* the man is not there

(iii) *pronominal subject without* ꞽw

〰 *nn* is used *with the dependent pronoun:*

e.g. 〰 𓃀𓈖𓏏𓅓 *nn sw ꞽm* he is not there

(iv) *pronominal subject with* ꞽw

꜀꜀꜀ *n* is used, and is placed before *ꞽw*:

e.g. ꜀꜀꜀ 𓇋𓅱𓆑𓅓 *n ꞽw.f ꞽm* he is not there

The copula

Sometimes, the subject and predicate of a non-verbal sentence can be linked together by a *copula* (a Latin word that means 'link'). In English translation, this link between subject and predicate is represented by the verb 'to be'.

In Egyptian, the copula is represented either by 𓇋𓅱 *ꞽw*, an old verb that in Middle Egyptian had been reduced to the meaning 'is', 'are'; or 𓃹𓈖 *wnn* (or 𓃹 *wn*), a verb that means 'exist'. When *ꞽw*, or *wnn* or *wn*, is used as a copula, it has no real verbal meaning but is used merely as a grammatical device. *Most non-verbal sentences are imprecise as to time, and can be translated as past, present or future, according to context.* The use of the copula helps to remedy this.

N.B. A copula is normally used only in sentences with adverbial predicate.

A. 𓇋𓅱 *ꞽw*

As we saw above, *ꞽw* was used either to give importance to a non-verbal sentence with adverbial predicate and noun subject; or to provide a support for a suffix-pronoun subject.

B. 𓃹𓈖 *wnn*

wnn is used *to mark the future:*

e.g. 𓃹𓈖𓆑𓎡𓇌 *wnn.f ḥnꜥ.ꞽ* he will be with me

C. 𓃹𓈖 *wn*

wn has three main uses:

(i) in subordinate clauses of time:

e.g. 𓃹𓈖𓇋𓅓𓇾𓊪𓈖 *wn.ꞽ m tꜣ pn* when I was in this land

(ii) in subordinate clauses of purpose:

e.g. 𓏶𓈖𓅱𓈖𓐠𓄿𓎡 ⟨hieroglyphs⟩

ῑ?.n.ῑ wn.ῑ m s3.k I have come so that I may be your protection

(iii) after the particle 𓇋𓄿 *ῑḫ* (see page 6):

e.g. ⟨hieroglyphs⟩

ῑḫ wn.ῑ m šms n nṯr may I be in the following of the god

D. The combination of 𓇋𓅱 with 𓃹𓈖 —*ῑw wn*—means 'there is' or 'there was':

e.g. ⟨hieroglyphs⟩ *ῑw wn s m pr* there was (or 'is') a man in the house

E. The combination of 𓂜𓈖 with 𓃹𓈖 —*nn wn*—means 'there is not' or 'there was not'
(lit: there exists/existed not):

e.g. ⟨hieroglyphs⟩ *nn wn mῑtt.f* there is no one like him (lit: there exists not
his like)

N.B. The phrase 𓂜𓈖 𓃹𓈖 does *not* conform to the rule that *nn sḏm.f* has future
meaning.

EXERCISE 7

(a) *Write in hieroglyphs and transliteration*

    1. It is true (i.e. the truth, n.) that he is our lord.

    2. The woman is a bad servant, she is not in her master's house.

    3. The scribe is not in his house.

    4. I was a follower of the Lord of the Two Lands.

    5. There is a shrine in the temple but there is no god in it.

(b) *Translate into English*

    1. ⟨hieroglyphs⟩

    2. ⟨hieroglyphs⟩

    3. ⟨hieroglyphs⟩

    4. ⟨hieroglyphs⟩

    5. ⟨hieroglyphs⟩

Chapter 8

VERBS: INTRODUCTION

Sentences and clauses

When we speak or write, we express our thoughts in groups of words called sentences, which may be subdivided into further groups of words called phrases and clauses. The essential requirements for any group of words to qualify as a sentence are that it *must* contain a *finite verb*; and express a *complete* action or thought.

A verb is a word that states an action; a *finite verb* is defined or limited in what it expresses by being qualified by a 'person' or 'number':

e.g. 'I go', where 'I' is the 1st person and the number singular; 'she goes', where 'she' is the 3rd person and the number singular; 'we go', where 'we' is the 1st person and the number plural; 'they go', where 'they' is the 3rd person and the number plural.

An *infinite verb* is one which merely states the action expressed by the verb without reference to any person or number: for instance, 'going', 'gone', 'to go'; 'walking', 'walked', 'to walk'; 'hitting', 'hit', 'to hit':

e.g. 'she goes to town every day' is a sentence because the verb 'goes' is qualified by the 3rd person singular 'she' and is therefore a finite verb.

'going to town every day', on the other hand, is not a sentence because no reference is made to any person or number; 'going', therefore, is an infinite verb.

A *phrase* is a group of words that on its own does not make complete sense and has to be attached to another group of words such as a sentence in order to do so:

e.g. 'very soon, we shall reach home': 'very soon' is a phrase because on its own it does not make complete sense, although it does so when attached to the sentence 'we shall reach home'; 'running down the street, the girl reached the house': 'running down the street' is a phrase because it makes complete sense only when attached to 'the girl reached the house'.

From the second example quoted above, it can be seen that a phrase may contain a verb. The essential difference, however, between the verb in a phrase and the verb in a sentence is that the former is always an infinite verb and the latter always a finite verb.

To sum up: the difference between a phrase and a sentence is that a phrase *never* contains a finite verb, although it may contain an infinite verb, whereas a sentence *must* contain a finite verb; and that a sentence makes complete sense on its own whereas a phrase does not.

A sentence is often made up of several *clauses.* A clause is a group of words that contains a *finite* verb but may or may not make complete sense on its own:

e.g. 'the girl came to the house where her mother lived':

> (i) 'the girl came to the house' contains a finite verb (came, defined by the subject, girl) and makes complete sense on its own.
>
> (ii) 'where her mother lived' contains a finite verb (lived, subject mother) but does not make complete sense in itself: it needs the addition of the first clause in order to do so.

Clause (i) above could stand on its own and make complete sense, but because it has been used with another clause that does not make complete sense on its own but depends on clause (i) in order to do so, clause (i) is called the *Main Clause.*

Clause (ii) above is dependent on the Main Clause (i) for its sense, it is subordinate to it. Clause (ii), therefore, is called the *Dependent* or *Subordinate Clause.*

When a dependent clause is considered in relation to a main clause, it can be seen that the dependent clause is playing the part of an adverb, an adjective or a noun:

e.g.   (i) Jack sang a song *when he had built the house*

      (ii) This is the house *that Jack built*

      (iii) Jack is the man *who built the house*

N.B. The words in italic make up the dependent clauses in each example.

In sentence (i) above, the clause 'when he had built the house' elaborates upon the verb 'sang' by telling us *when* Jack sang a song. Since an adverb is a word that describes a verb, the dependent clause in this case is called an *adverbial clause.* In sentence (ii), the clause 'that Jack built' describes the noun 'house'. An adjective is a word that describes a noun; the dependent clause in this case, therefore, is called an *adjectival clause.* In sentence (iii), the clause 'who built the house' qualifies the noun, 'man'; in this case, therefore, the dependent clause is called a *noun clause.*

In the following Chapters, we shall see how the Egyptians expressed various types of clause. At this point, it will suffice if the Reader learns that in Egyptian there are two types of subordinate or dependent clause: one that is introduced by a preposition or other introductory word; and one that is not and simply consists of two clauses juxtaposed with the translator left to supply the appropriate English word (see IEH, p. 103). The former type of clause is called a Real Subordinate Clause and the latter a Virtual Subordinate Clause.

Although Virtual Subordinate Clauses are more common in Egyptian, they can be found in English also:

e.g. 'I am reading the book you gave me' is an abbreviated rendering of the grammatically more correct 'I am reading the book *that* you gave *to* me.'

In both examples, 'I am reading the book' is the main clause, but in the first example, the dependent clause 'you gave me' has been directly juxtaposed to it, making a virtual subordinate clause, whereas in the second example, the dependent clause is introduced by the adjective 'that', making a real subordinate clause.

Verbs in English

In IEH (Lesson 8), we learned that a verb is a word that tells us what somebody or something does. A verb can also tell us what someone thinks, and is therefore the word in a sentence that states an action or a thought. In English, verbs can be, as we have seen (page 51) Infinite or Finite. They can also have Tenses, Moods, an Active Voice and a Passive Voice.

Verbs—Tenses

Every action stated by every verb must take place now, or in the future; or it must have taken place in the past. The *Tense* is the form of the verb chosen to express the time at which the action of the verb takes, has taken or will take place. There are three tenses:

Present Tense: he runs

Past Tense: he ran

Future Tense: he will run.

The tenses of a verb can be further elaborated to indicate whether the action of the verb has been completed or is still going on. An action that is now finished is expressed by the Perfect Tense ('perfect' here means completed). An action that is still going on is expressed by the Continuous Tense.

The Tenses of a verb may be tabulated thus:

	Present	*Past*	*Future*
Simple	I run	I ran	I shall run
Continuous	I am running	I was running	I shall be running
Perfect	I have run	I had run	I shall have run

N.B. The Past Perfect Tense is sometimes called the Pluperfect. The Past Continuous Tense is sometimes called the Imperfect

Verbs—Mood

The *Mood* of a verb is the form of the verb that serves to show *the way* in which the action is being performed. There are four moods:

(1) Indicative: used positively to state facts or ask questions:

e.g. 'she went home'; 'is she going home?'

(2) Subjunctive: used to express a wish, a doubt, a hope, an uncertainty:

e.g. 'may I go home?'; 'if only I could go home'.

(3) Imperative: used to command, request, beg:

e.g. 'go home!'; 'will you go home!'

(4) Infinitive: used to show an action or a state, without reference

to a subject: e.g. 'to go home'; 'going home'.

Verbs—Voice—active and passive

The subject of a verb is the person or thing performing the action of the verb. When a verb is in the *Active Voice*, it is referring to things done *by* the subject of the verb: e.g. 'John hit Jane' where John (subject) is the *doer* of the action of the verb (hit). When a verb is the *Passive Voice*, it is referring to things done *to* the subject of the verb: e.g. 'John was hit by Jane' where the subject (John) of the verb (hit) is the *receiver* of the action of the verb. 'Jane' is the *agent* through whom the action is carried out.

Verbs in Egyptian

In Egyptian, there are ways of writing verbs (called 'the verb-form') that clearly indicate Passive or Active Voice. Tense and Mood, however, are not so clearly indicated; and even Voice is sometimes not distinguished. In these cases, one has to translate the verb into English according to what seems best considering the context in which it is found (see IEH, p. 97).

In English, the various tenses, voices, etc., are formed by adding or subtracting syllables to the basic verb-stem, or by using auxiliary (i.e. helping) verbs such as 'be', 'do', 'have', or by altering letters in the basic verb-stem. This basic verb-stem is formed from the present tense of the verb.

e.g. the verbs 'laugh' and 'forget':

Present	I laugh	he forget*s*
Past	I laugh*ed*	he forg*o*t
Future	I *shall* laugh	he *will* forget

In Egyptian, the verb-stem forms the basis on to which all the elements that make up the various tenses etc. can be added. In IEH, the Reader was introduced to the verb-form *sḏm.f.* At that time, it was not necessary for him to be told that the stem of the verb was *not* unchangeable. At this point, however, the time has come for the Reader to learn that Egyptian verbs are divided into classes according to the *number* and *kind* of consonants from which the stem is made up; and that the behaviour of some of the verbs in the different classes is an indication of tense and mood.

We must suppose that the Egyptians themselves differentiated between certain tenses and moods in their spoken language by stressing certain consonants or adding vowel sounds. But alas, in the *written* language, only consonants were drawn; hence, the hieroglyphic writing of, for instance, ⬛🦆 *sḏm.f* consisting as it does of consonants only, might embody a variety of pronunciations and therefore of verb-forms: sedemef; esedjemef; seddamef, etc.

All that we can see in the written language is that Egyptian verbs are written in consonants (which we call *radicals*), and that the stems of most verbs consist of three consonants, although some have two and others have four, five or six.

The reader who wishes to learn in detail about verb classes in Middle Egyptian should consult Gardiner, 'Egyptian Grammar', Chapter XXI. For our purposes, it is sufficient to simplify Egyptian verbs into three groups as follows:

(1) Those in which the *last* radical is *neither* a semi-vowel (🦅 *w* or 𓏭 *ỉ*) *nor* identical with the penultimate radical. These verbs are called *strong* or *immutable* (unchanging) *verbs*;

e.g.   ⬛⬛ *mn* 'be firm'   ⬛🦆 *sḏm* 'hear'

🦅⬛⬛ *wstn* 'stride'   𓏤𓊨 *s'nḥ* 'make live'

⬛⬛⬛ *nftft* 'spring away'

𓏤⬛⬛⬛ *swtwt* 'walk', 'promenade'

(2) Those whose stem ends in one of the semi-vowels *w* or *ỉ* (note that *w* and *ỉ* are often omitted in writing). These verbs are called *weak verbs*;

e.g.   ⬛⬛ *ršw* 'rejoice'   ⬛⬛⬛ *s3w* 'guard', 'prevent'

⬛⬛ *g3w* 'be narrow'   ⬛⬛ *mrỉ* 'love', 'wish'

⬛ *ỉrỉ* 'make', 'do'

⬛⬛⬛ *hwy* (sometimes transliterated *ḥỉỉ*) 'strike'

(3) Those whose stem ends in two *identical* radicals. These verbs are called *geminating verbs* because the penultimate radical is doubled or twinned (geminated):

e.g.   ⬛⬛⬛ *3mm* 'seize', 'grip'

⬛⬛ *wnn* 'be', 'exist'

wrr 'be great'

m33 'see'

rnn 'nurse'

hnn 'bow', 'assent to'

ẖnn 'destroy'

šmm 'be hot'

šrr 'be small' (later ⟨glyphs⟩ šrỉ)

ḳbb 'be cool'

gnn 'be soft'

tkk 'attack', 'violate (a frontier)'

N.B. There are three verbs (⟨glyphs⟩ snbb 'converse'; ⟨glyphs⟩ spdd 'supply'; ⟨glyphs⟩ špss 'be rich') that appear to be geminating verbs. *They are not*, they are derived from the adjectives snb 'healthy', spd 'ready' and šps 'noble' respectively, and are *immutable* (see section (1) above).

EXERCISE 8

Learn the geminating verbs given above so that you can distinguish between those verbs that *always* geminate (and form the geminating class), and those verbs that only geminate in certain circumstances (see below, pages 59, 137).

Chapter 9

VERBS: PRESENT TENSE

Active voice

The sense of the English Simple, Continuous and Perfect Present Tenses (see page 54)
Active Voice can be conveyed in Egyptian, in both main and subordinate clauses, by
using the *sḏm.f* verb-form (see IEH, p. 97):

e.g. [hieroglyphs]

sḥs st r pr

the woman *runs* into the house (Simple Present Tense)

or

the woman *is running* into the house (Continuous Present Tense)

or

the woman *has run* into the house (Perfect Present Tense)

Note that in the examples given above, the *stem* of the verb remains unchanged no
matter what tense is being indicated. However, in certain circumstances, the stem of the
sḏm.f verb-form does change: the weak verbs sometimes geminate (see page 137; and
below, page 59). Note also that the Present Perfect Tense can also be rendered by the
sḏm.n.f verb-form (see below, page 66).

The *sḏm.f* in subordinate clauses

Virtual subordinate clauses

1. In virtual subordinate clauses (see page 53), the *sḏm.f* is most often used in a virtual
   clause of *purpose* (that is, a clause that in English is introduced by the words 'that', 'in

order that', 'so that'):

e.g. 𓂋𓊨𓏭�... *h3b.k sš dd.f shr.k*

h3b.k sš ḏd.f sḥr.k

lit: you send the scribe he says your plan

i.e. you send the scribe so that he may tell of your plan

wp.ỉ r.ỉ mdw.ỉ

lit: I open my mouth I speak

i.e. I open my mouth in order that I may speak

2. The *sḏm.f* is also used in virtual clauses of *circumstance,* that is, in subordinate clauses which describe the time or circumstance in which the action of the main clause is taking place:

e.g. you will see Re *shining in the sky*

    they rejoiced *when they saw him*

    while I was in the house, I did not sleep

(the words in italics are subordinate clauses of circumstance). It should be noted that clauses of circumstance are *always* subordinate clauses, *never* main clauses.

It is thought that originally, in Egyptian, weak verbs being used in clauses of circumstance geminated. However, in Middle Egyptian, this was no longer always the case, and examples have been found which show no gemination but which must be translated into English as clauses of circumstance. In fact, such examples appear to be more numerous than those which show gemination.

e.g. 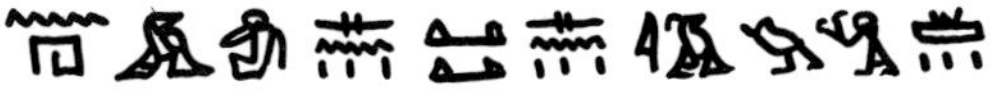 *nhm.sn ḏd.sn ỉ3w*

    they rejoice while they give acclamation

where the verb in the subordinate clause (𓂝𓂝�) is the geminating form of the verb

𓂝𓂝 *rdỉ* 'give', 'reveal';

but *m3.k rꜥ dỉ.f sw ḥr nnt*

    you see Re when he shows himself in the heavens

where the verb in the subordinate clause (𓂝𓂝) is the non-geminating form of *rdỉ*.

3. The *sḏm.f* can also be used in a virtual clause of *condition*, that is, in a subordinate clause that in English is introduced by 'whether'. Alternative conditions are often posed—'whether . . . or whether' clauses: in such cases, Egyptian *repeats the verb*:

e.g. [hieroglyphs]

m3.sn pt m3.sn t3 mk3 'ib.sn

(whether) they looked at the sky (or whether) they looked at the earth, their hearts were brave

[hieroglyphs]

h3.f r pt h3.f r t3 h3.f r mw sh̬n.f 3bwt.f

whether he ascends to the sky or descends to the earth or plunges into water, he will rejoin his family

Real subordinate clauses

The use of a preposition, conjunction, etc., to introduce the *sḏm.f* in a subordinate clause enables the meaning of the clause to be more precisely indicated. In real subordinate clauses (see page 53), the *sḏm.f* (Present Tense) is often introduced by (1) *prepositions*, the most commonly used of which are [gly] *m*, [gly] *ḥr*, [gly] *ḥft* and [gly] *mi*; and by (2) the particle [gly] *'ir*.

(1) *sḏm.f after prepositions*

[gly]   *m* 'when':   the boy eats [hieroglyphs] *m ḥḳr.f*
                         when he is hungry
                         (in English, an adverbial clause of time)

[gly]   *ḥr* 'because': his heart is happy [hieroglyphs] *ḥr m33.f wi*
                         because he sees me
                         (in English, an adverbial clause of reason)

𓄿   *ḥft* 'when'   my heart is happy 𓄿𓅱𓎡𓉐𓂝 *ḥft m3.ỉ st* when I
see her

(in English, an adverbial clause of time)

𓐙𓏤   *mỉ* 'as when',   it is done 𓐙𓏤����𓏤𓊪 *mỉ dd nb.ỉ*

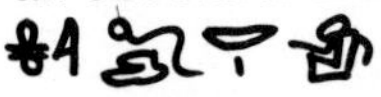

       'according   according as my master says

       as'   (in English, an adverbial clause of manner)

(2) *sḏm.f* after 𓇋𓂋 *ỉr*

The particle 𓇋𓂋 *ỉr* followed by a *geminating sḏm.f* is as a rule taken to be a clause
of *circumstance*:

e.g. 𓇋𓂋𓄿𓄿𓄿𓂋𓏤𓏤𓈖𓏤𓂝𓂋𓏤𓆱𓏤𓊪

   ỉr gmm.k bbwy.f(y) sd ḥr.s

   when you find his collar-bone broken because of it

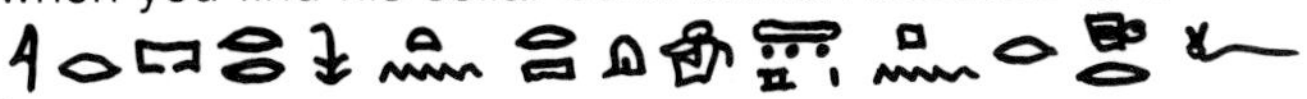

𓇋𓂋𓉐𓏏𓏤𓈖𓆷𓅱𓇾𓈖𓂋𓂧𓂋𓆑

   ỉr prr nsw ršw t3 pn r-ḏr.f

   when the king goes forth, the whole land rejoices

Note that the verbs above, *gmm* and *prr*, are showing gemination although they
do not belong to the class of geminating verbs (see page 56). This is because
when weak verbs (see page 56) are used after the particle *ỉr*, they usually
geminate, that is, they drop the weak final radical *ỉ* or *w* and double the strong
penultimate radical (in the examples above, *m* and *r*), *in order to indicate a clause
of circumstance*. If a weak verb does *not* geminate after *ỉr*, it is usually taken to
be the introduction to a conditional clause (see below page 74).

Passive voice

The Passive Voice of the Present Tense is formed from the *sḏm.f* verb-form by adding
the element 𓂝𓆓 (sometimes written 𓆓𓂝) *tw* immediately after the verb-stem, from

which it is *never* separated, thus making up the 𓊃𓏤𓂋𓄿 *sḏm.tw.f* verb-form. The paradigm of the *sḏm.tw.f* is given below:

singular

1st pers. c.	𓊃𓏤𓂋𓅱𓀁	*sḏm.tw.ỉ*	I am heard
2nd pers. m.	𓊃𓏤𓂋𓎡	*sḏm.tw.k*	you are heard
2nd pers. f.	𓊃𓏤𓂋𓏏	*sḏm.tw.t*	you are heard
3rd pers. m.	𓊃𓏤𓂋𓆑	*sḏm.tw.f*	he is heard
3rd pers. f.	𓊃𓏤𓂋𓋴	*sḏm.tw.s*	she is heard

plural

1st pers. c.	𓊃𓏤𓂋𓏤𓏤𓏤	*sḏm.tw.n*	we are heard
2nd pers. c.	𓊃𓏤𓂋𓏏𓈖	*sḏm.tw.ṯn*	you are heard
3rd pers. c.	𓊃𓏤𓂋𓋴𓏤𓏤𓏤	*sḏm.tw.sn*	they are heard

Note 1. When the subject of the *sḏm.tw.f* is a *pronoun*, it is *never* separated from the verb-stem plus *tw*:

e.g. 𓂋𓂧𓏏𓆑𓈖 *rdỉ.tw.f n.f* it is given to him

However, when the subject of the *sḏm.tw.f* is a *noun,* then it can, under certain circumstances, be separated from the combination of verb-stem plus *tw*. The normal rules of the word order (see IEH, p. 102) dictate when this can happen:

e.g. 𓆓𓂧𓏏𓆑𓈖𓂋𓏤 *ḏd.tw.n.f r pn* this utterance is said to him

where *r* (utterance) is the noun subject of the verb (*ḏd.tw*) but *n.f* (to him) is the datival 𓈖 *n* plus a suffix-pronoun, which must precede a noun; the subject of the *sḏm.tw.f*, *r*, must therefore be separated from the verb-stem plus passive element 𓂧𓏏.

Note 2. The passive element 𓂧𓏏 *tw* is really an indefinite pronoun, like 'one' in English or 'on' in French; and it can be used in impersonal statements. For instance, 𓆓𓂧𓏏 *ḏd.tw*. At first glance, this looks like a *sḏm.tw.f* with subject missing. Be on the look out for occasions when this is not so and where *ḏd.tw* is to be translated 'one says' or 'it is said' (impersonal use).

N.B. The King was often referred to impersonally; in such cases, *ḏd.tw* would be translated as 'One says', where 'One' is the King.

Note 3. Sometimes, a shorter writing, ⌒ , is found instead of ⌒𓂝 *tw*: this should always be borne in mind to avoid confusion with other verb-forms (see pages 86, 93, 126, 127, 129).

The position is more clear when verbs are written with *determinatives.* When the element that forms the passive (*tw*) is written *after* the determinative, the full form is used normally:

e.g. 𓂋𓐍𓏏𓅱 *rḫ.tw.f* he is known

When the passive element *tw* is written *before* the determinative, it is often the short form (⌒) that is used:

e.g. 𓂋𓐍𓏏𓅱 *rḫ.t(w).f* he is known

(Note the transliteration *t(w)*)

There seems to be no hard and fast rule as to whether to place the passive element *tw* before or after the determinative, but it should be remembered that hieroglyphs were a decorative script, and that if the exigencies of space demanded a shorter line of hieroglyphic signs, then the abbreviated writing ⌒ might be chosen; and then placed *before* the determinative for safety, so that it did not become lost amongst the following hieroglyphs.

Unfortunately, the shorter form, ⌒ , is sometimes written *after* a determinative!

e.g. 𓂋𓐍𓏏 *rḫ.t(w).f.* It is this writing of the *sḏm.tw.f* that can most easily be confused with other verb-forms (see above).

The Agent

Consider the sentence 'this utterance is being spoken by a man'. 'this utterance' is the subject of the verb 'being spoken' which is in the passive voice; 'a man' is the *agent*, that is, the person performing the action of the verb. In Egyptian, the agent is expressed after the *sḏm.tw.f,* or indeed, after the passive of any verb form, by the preposition 𓇋𓈖 *in* 'by':

e.g. [hieroglyphs]

<u>d</u>d.tw r pn <u>i</u>n s this utterance is being spoken by a man

Uses of the s<u>d</u>m.tw.f

The s<u>d</u>m.tw.f is used in both main and subordinate clauses in the same way as the s<u>d</u>m.f (see page 58). For example, in a subordinate clause of purpose:

[hieroglyphs]

h3b.tw sš <u>d</u>d.tw s<u>h</u>r.k

One is sending the scribe *so that your plan might be told*, where the words in italics constitute a virtual clause of purpose.

EXERCISE 9

(a) *Write in hieroglyphs and transliteration*
    1. I am sending a boat to the city so that you may be ferried across in it.
    2. One eats bread because one is hungry.
    3. The servants are happy when they drink beer.
    4. The whole land rejoices when the gods are seen in their beautiful places of the West.
    5. She knows the name of that god who is in this temple.

(b) *Translate into English*
    1. [hieroglyphs]
    2. [hieroglyphs]
    3. [hieroglyphs]
    4. [hieroglyphs]
    5. [hieroglyphs]

Chapter 10

VERBS: PAST TENSE

Active voice

The sense of the English Past Simple and Past Perfect (Pluperfect) Tenses (see page 54) Active Voice can be conveyed in Egyptian by a verb-form known as the *sḏm.n.f*. The *sḏm.n.f*, which can be used in both main and subordinate clauses, normally refers to an action that has taken place in the past and that has now finished completely. It is, therefore, *not* used to convey the sense of the English Past Continuous (Imperfect) Tense (see page 54).

The ⬦𝄪🐒〰 *sḏm.n.f* is written exactly like the *sḏm.f* form except that the element 〰 *n* is placed *immediately after* the verb-stem, or after any determinatives the verb-stem may have. An abbreviated paradigm is set out below:

singular

1st pers. c.	⬦𝄪〰𓏤	*sḏm.n.ỉ*	I heard (or had heard)
2nd pers. m.	⬦𝄪〰⌒	*sḏm.n.k*	you heard (or had heard)
2nd pers. f.	⬦𝄪〰⊃	*sḏm.n.t*	you heard (or had heard)

N.B. The 1st person singular suffix (𓏤 *ỉ*) is often omitted in writing. The element, 〰 , *n*, is inseparable from the verb-stem and comes between it and the subject of the verb, even when that subject is a suffix-pronoun:

e.g. 𝄃𝄃ᴧ〰 *ỉỉ.n.s*   she came
𝄃𝄃ᴧ 𓏤𓂝 *ỉỉ.n nsw*   the king came

The above examples have been translated as Past Simple Tenses.

They could equally well have been translated as Past Perfect: 'she had come', 'the king had come'.

Peculiarities of the *sḏm.n.f* form

(1) The *sḏm.n.f* can be translated, where context demands it, as *Present* Perfect (see page 54):

e.g. 🏛🐍𓀀 ◡ 〰 ◡ 𓏤 ◡

   h3b.n n.k nb.k your lord has sent to you

It will be noted from the example above that when the subject of the *sḏm.n.f* is a noun, the normal rules of word order apply. In this case, the noun subject (*nb.k* 'your lord') has been separated from the verb-stem plus the element 〰 because a dative plus suffix-pronoun (*n.k*) must come before a noun subject (see IEH, p. 102).

(2) In texts accompanying ritual scenes, the *first person singular* of the *sḏm.n.f* is often found where one might expect the *sḏm.f*; in other words, where the verb obviously has to be translated as a present rather than a past tense. In these scenes, the action is usually being spoken of *and* performed at the same time (synchronous present):

e.g. △〰 〰 ⚚ 𓀀 ◡

   dỉ.n.(ỉ) n.k 'nḫ w3s nb

   I (omitted in the hieroglyphs; see above p. 65) give you all life and dominion (words spoken by a god to a king in a temple relief).

(3) The verbs ⊘ *rḫ* 'know' and 𓏤𓃻𓂋𓏭 *sḫ3* 'remember' often, but not always, have present meaning in their *sḏm.n.f* forms. This is because the Egyptians considered 'knowing' to be the same as 'having learned' and 'remembering' as 'having recollected'—processes which have been completed; hence the use of *sḏm.n.f*, the tense of completed action, as a present tense:

e.g. ⊘〰𓏤𓏤𓏤 𓂝 ◡𓊪𓏤𓏤𓏤

   rḫ.n.sn ỉnk nb.sn they know I am their lord

   𓏤𓃻𓂋𓏭〰𓊪𓂝〰𓋴𓏤 ।

   sḫ3.n.ỉ rn n s I remember the name of the man.

The Past Continuous Tense

The *sḏm.n.f* form is *not* used to render the sense of the English Past *Continuous* Tense;

as we saw on page 65, the *sḏm.n.f* was used only to express actions which have been *completed*. In Egyptian, the Past Continuous Tense is expressed by the *sḏm.f* form, once again illustrating the uncertain boundaries between the verb forms:

e.g. 𓂋𓅓 𓊪 𓍿 𓁷𓏤 𓈖𓏏𓏏 𓏃𓎡𓂋𓇋𓊃

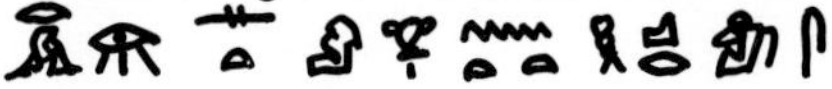

rm st ḥr-ntt ḥkr.s the woman was crying because she was hungry

The *sḏm.n.f* in main clauses

In main clauses, the *sḏm.n.f* is most commonly used as a *past narrative* tense, that is, to tell about things which happened in the past:

e.g. 𓉔�paⳛ𓀀 𓈖𓈖 𓎟𓀀𓏤 𓂋 𓆎𓏏𓊖

h3b.n wi nb.i r kmt my lord sent me to Egypt

𓉔𓂧𓈖𓆑 𓁷𓏤𓆑 𓄣𓆑 𓄿𓅱

ḥd.n.f ḥr.f ib.f 3w he travelled down over it (a canal) his heart being glad

The compound form 𓇋𓅱 𓄔𓂝𓅓 𓈖 *iw sḏm.n.f*

The word 𓇋𓅱 *iw* placed before the *sḏm.n.f* form *in main clauses* was a device often used by the Egyptians to mark an important event in the narrative. In some cases, it is an indication *to the translator* to begin a new paragraph, something which would not otherwise be obvious in a continuous run of hieroglyphs, since the Egyptians used no punctuation:

e.g. After a long description of a giant serpent, the narrator continues with what is obviously an important event in his story:

𓇋𓅱𓊪𓈖𓆑 𓂋𓆑 𓂋𓀀

iw wp.n.f r.f r.i he opened his mouth to me.

The *sḏm.n.f* in subordinate clauses

Virtual subordinate clauses

Like the *sḏm.f* (see p. 58), the *sḏm.n.f* can be found in virtual subordinate clauses. This is particularly common with virtual clauses of *time*, that is, clauses that in English are introduced by 'when', 'after', 'until', 'since', 'before', etc.:

e.g. 〔hieroglyphs〕

　　ḥḏ.n t3 sḥr ḥm.f ḥftyw.f when day dawned, his Majesty overthrew his enemies

Real subordinate clauses

It is more common for the *sḏm.n.f* to be found in real subordinate clauses. In such clauses, the only prepositions used to introduce the *sḏm.n.f* are 〔hieroglyphs〕 m-ḥt; 〔hieroglyph〕 r; 〔hieroglyphs〕 mỉ; 〔hieroglyphs〕 ḥft:

e.g. 〔hieroglyphs〕 m-ḥt 'after', 'when':

　　〔hieroglyphs〕

　　wḏ3.n ḥm.f m ḥtp m-ḥt sḥr.n.f ḥftyw.f

　　his Majesty proceeded in peace after he had overthrown his enemies

　　〔hieroglyph〕 r 'until':

　　his Majesty proceeded in peace 〔hieroglyphs〕 r spr.n.f r nỉwt until he reached the city

　　〔hieroglyphs〕 mỉ 'like', 'as':

　　〔hieroglyphs〕

　　ỉr.n.f ḳrs mỉ ỉr.n Ḥr n ỉt.f

　　he performed the burial as Horus did (or 'had done') for his father

　　〔hieroglyphs〕 ḥft 'according to', 'according as':

　　〔hieroglyphs〕

　　ỉr.n ḥm.f ḥft mr.n.f

　　his Majesty acted according as he desired

Passive voice—the passive *sḏm.f* form

We have seen that *sḏm.f* is present tense, active voice; that *sḏm.n.f* is past tense, active voice; and that *sḏm.tw.f* is present tense, passive voice. It is tempting, therefore, to say that the passive voice of the past tense must be formed by adding the particle ▱𓅱 *tw* to *sḏm.n.f*, giving *sḏm.n.tw.f* This is not the case!

The normal passive of the past tense is a construction called the *passive sḏm.f form*. When written with a *suffix-pronoun* as subject, the passive *sḏm.f* form often looks exactly the same as the active *sḏm.f*. Sometimes, however, the ending 𓇌 *y* is used, especially with verbs that have a final weak radical:

e.g. 𓄟𓇌𓅱 *msy.i* I was born (from 𓄟𓋴𓇋 *msi* 'give birth')

𓐍𓇌𓂧 *iṯy.k* you were seized (from 𓐍𓏏𓂡 *iṯi* 'seize')

When written with a *noun* as subject, the passive *sḏm.f* form *can* have 𓅱 *w* (var. 𓏲) as an ending:

e.g. 𓈙𓅱𓂧𓏏𓆑 *š'w drt.f* his hand was cut off

𓎛𓅱𓋴𓅱 ~~~ 𓈖𓇋 𓉴 *ḥwsw n.i mr* a pyramid was constructed for me

N.B. The ending 𓅱 *w* (or 𓏲) is written *before* the determinative of the verb, if any.

In older grammars, the passive *sḏm.f* was called the *sḏmw.f* form, a term which is not strictly accurate since the *w* was never written before suffix-pronoun subjects, only before noun subjects. Although at first sight it seems that it would be easy to confuse the passive *sḏm.f* form with active *sḏm.f*, in practice *context* invariably determines that it be translated with passive meaning.

Use of the passive *sḏm.f* form

The passive *sḏm.f* form is restricted in its use. It is *not* normally used in subordinate clauses (its place in these being taken by the Stative, see below p. 92); and it is seldom used with a pronominal subject, although it is often used in an impersonal way i.e. with a third person pronoun subject *understood but not written*:

e.g.   🗚🗚🗚 *smỉw*   it was reported

🗚🗚 *ỉrw*   it was done

🗚🗚🗚🗚🗚🗚🗚 *ỉrw ḥft wḏ.n ḥm.f* it was done according as his Majesty commanded

The chief use of the passive *sḏm.f* form is with *noun subject in a main clause:*

e.g.   🗚🗚🗚🗚🗚

rdỉw n.k t3w   breath has been given to you

🗚🗚🗚🗚

šsp(w) ḥrpw   the mallet has been taken

The 🗚🗚🗚 *sḏm.ỉn.f* as a past narrative tense

The *sḏm.ỉn.f* is a verb-form that is made up from the stem of the verb followed by the formative element 🗚 *ỉn* (appended *after* the determinative, if any) both of which are inseparable from each other. If the subject of the verb is *pronominal*, then it is expressed by the suffix-pronoun appended directly after *ỉn* and, according to rule, never separated from it. However, if the subject is a *noun*, then under certain conditions (see page 131) it may be separated from the verb-stem plus *ỉn*:

e.g.   🗚🗚🗚🗚 *sḏm.ỉn.ỉ*   I heard

🗚🗚🗚🗚 *ḏd.ỉn.ỉ*   I said

🗚🗚🗚🗚 *ḥʿ.ỉn.sn*   they rejoiced

(note position of determinative)

The passive form is made up in the same way as the active form with the addition of the passive element 🗚🗚 *tw* placed *directly after ỉn* from which it is never separated:

e.g.   🗚🗚🗚🗚 *ỉr.ỉn.tw.f* he was brought

Uses of the *sḏm.ỉn.f* form

The *sḏm.ỉn.f* is found *in main clauses only*, where it is often used to introduce some outstanding event that has taken place in the past:

e.g. [hieroglyphs]

ḏd.ỉn ḥm n nsw-bỉt

then spoke the majesty of the King of Upper and Lower Egypt

[hieroglyphs]

ỉn.ỉn.tw.f n.f ḥr-ꜥwy

then he was brought to him immediately

EXERCISE 10

(a) *Write in hieroglyphs and transliteration*

1. The hungry man was given bread by my lord.

2. I made this temple for my father, Amun.

3. When he had arrived at the city, he found no-one.

4. She saw the priest after she had entered the temple.

5. My lord knows that I am a good servant.

(b) *Translate into English*

1. [hieroglyphs]

2. [hieroglyphs]

3. [hieroglyphs]

4. [hieroglyphs]

5. [hieroglyphs]

Chapter 11

VERBS: FUTURE TENSE

Active Voice

The Future Tense (Active Voice) in Egyptian is often expressed simply by the *sḏm.f* form:

e.g. 𓂝𓀁𓂋 𓊪𓉐

    m3.k pr.k you will see your home

𓏠𓋴𓇋𓄿𓈖𓄿𓊮𓏤𓉐𓏤

    ms.s m 3bd 1 (n) prt she will give birth in the first month of winter

However, it is possible to indicate a Future Tense more precisely by using a special form of the *sḏm.f* called the *Prospective sḏm.f*, whose very name 'Prospective' means concerned with or applying to the future only.

    The Prospective *sḏm.f* may be distinguished from the ordinary *sḏm.f* form by a variety of special endings which are attached to the verb-stem and come between it and the subject of the verb, even when that subject is a suffix-pronoun. Unfortunately, these endings were not used consistently, and some verbs do not display any distinguishing marks at all. In these cases, only context determines whether the verb should be translated as a *sḏm.f* that is being used to indicate future tense or as a *sḏm.f* that is being used to indicate a present or past continuous tense (see page 54).

    The endings of the Prospective *sḏm.f* are: 𓇌 -*y* and 𓅱 -*w* (varr. 𓏲 , 𓏭 , 𓏮), although some verbs display the endings 𓏏 -*t* and 𓈖 -*n*.

(i)   𓇌 -*y* is found mainly with weak verbs, especially with the first person singular, but it is sometimes found with strong verbs:

    e.g.   𓁹   *ỉrỉ*   'do' has Prospective form   𓁹𓇌   *ỉry*

          𓌸𓂋   *mrỉ*   'love' has Prospective form   𓌸𓂋𓇌   *mry*

          𓉔𓄿𓂢   *h3ỉ*   'go down' has Prospective form   𓉔𓄿𓇌   *h3y sʿ3* 'make great' has Prospective form *sʿ3y*

e.g. *ỉry.f* he will make

mry.s she will love

(ii) (varr. , ,) -*w* is found with both weak and strong verbs:

e.g. *sbỉ* 'go' has Prospective form *sbw*

ʿḥʿ 'stand' has Prospective form *ʿḥʿw*

ḫmsỉ 'sit' has Prospective form *ḫmsw*

snb 'recover' has Prospective form *snbw*

sḫwd 'enrich' has Prospective form *sḫwdw*

e.g. *ḫmsw.sn* they will sit

ʿḥʿw.k you will stand

(iii) -*t* has so far been found only with the verbs *ỉw* 'come' (Prospective form *ỉwt*) and *ỉnỉ* 'bring' (Prospective form *ỉnt*):

e.g. *ỉwt.ỉ* I shall come

ỉnt.n we will bring

(iv) -*n* is very commonly used with *m33* 'see', giving the Prospective form *m3n*:

e.g. *m3n.ṯn* you will see

The Prospective *sḏm.f* in main clauses

The Prospective *sḏm.f* can be used in main clauses in indicative mood, that is, to state facts or ask questions:

e.g. *hdy.n ptpt.n.n ḫ3swt* we will go north when we have crushed foreign lands

snbw.f ḥr.ʿwy he will recover immediately

ỉry.k n.f ỉsst what (*ỉsst*) will you do to him?

The Prospective *sḏm.f* in subordinate clauses

1. The Prospective *sḏm.f* is most often used in subordinate clauses of (i) condition and
   (ii) purpose, both real and virtual:
   (i) *conditional clauses* i.e. clauses that in English are introduced by 'if', 'unless',
       'whether', 'provided that', etc.:
       (a) *real* conditional clauses can be introduced by a particle such as 𓇋𓂋 *ỉr* 'if';
           𓈖𓏤𓇋𓂋 *mk ỉr* 'see, if', followed by the verb in its Prospective form, if it has
           one:

           e.g. 𓇋𓂋𓏤𓄿𓀁𓂝𓂋𓅓

           ỉr ỉwt.k r.ỉ if you come to me

           𓈖𓏤𓇋𓂋𓂋𓇋𓇋𓏤𓇳𓅓𓉐𓏤

           mk ỉr ỉry.f hrw m pr.ỉ see, if he spends a day in my house

       (b) *virtual* conditional clauses can contain the Prospective form of the verb without
           any introductory particle:

           e.g. 𓂋𓇋𓇋𓂋𓏥𓐍𓏏𓂝𓈖𓐍

           ỉry.k nn 3ḫ n.k if you do these things, it will be profitable to you

   (ii) *clauses of purpose* i.e. clauses that in English are introduced by 'that', 'so that', 'in
       order that':
       (a) *real* clauses of purpose can be introduced by prepositions such as 𓂋 *r* or
           particles such as 𓈖 𓏏𓏤𓀁 *n-mrwt*, followed by the verb in its Prospective
           form:

           e.g. 𓇋𓇋𓆑𓂋𓊪𓂋𓊹𓂋𓅓𓏱𓈖𓂝

           ỉỉ.f r pr-nṯr r m3n.f ỉt.f

           he comes to the temple in order that he may see his father

           𓋴𓏠𓈖𓐍𓈖𓏤𓏏𓈖𓏏𓏤𓏱𓇋𓇋𓂋𓂋𓏤𓏏

           smnḫ.n.ỉ tw n-mrwt ỉry.k n.ỉ ḫt

           I have endowed you in order that you may perform the rites for me

       (b) *virtual* clauses of purpose have no introductory word although the verb in the
           Prospective form is often an indication of how they should be translated:

e.g. [hieroglyphs]

rd̓w n.ỉ ỉrty.ỉ m3n.ỉ ỉm.sn

my eyes have been given to me in order that I may see by means of them

N.B. This sentence could have been *transliterated* as follows: *rd̓w n.ỉ ỉrty.ỉ m3.n.ỉ ỉm.sn* with the verb 'see' (*m3*) in the *sḏm.n.f* form rather than in the Prospective. In this case, it would have been translated 'my eyes were given to me. I saw by means of them'—an example of the fact that Egyptian hieroglyphs can be ambiguous!

2. The Prospective *sḏm.f* is used as the *object* of verbs of saying ([gly] *ḏd*); commanding ([gly] *wḏ*); wishing ([gly] *mr*); fearing ([gly] *snḏ*); knowing ([gly] *rḫ*):

e.g. [hieroglyphs]

wḏ.n ḥm.f sbw.f r pwnt

his Majesty commanded that he should go to Punt

[hieroglyphs]

ḏd.n.s sw ỉnt.f mw

she told him to bring water

or

she asked that he should bring water

[hieroglyphs]

rḫ.f ỉry.s st

he knows that she will do it

N.B. The verb [gly] *rd̓* 'give', 'place' can take as object another verb in the *sḏm.f* form; when it does so, *rd̓* then means 'cause' or 'allow':

e.g. [hieroglyphs]

d̓.ỉ sḏm.k

I allow you to hear *or* I cause you to hear

(lit: I give (that) you hear)

When *rd̓* is used with the meaning of 'cause', 'allow', the following verb is often in the Prospective *sḏm.f* form:

e.g.

rdỉ.n.f m3n.s sw

he allowed her to see him

(lit: he gave (that) she will see him)

rdỉ.n.ỉ ỉnt.f n.k 3tpw

I caused him to bring you a load

(lit: I gave (that) he will bring to you a load)

3. *The Prospective sḏm.f in Optative Clauses*

In Egyptian, it is difficult to distinguish clauses in the subjunctive mood, that is, clauses expressing a wish or a doubt (Optative Clauses) from those in the indicative mood expressing a command or an exhortation (see page 83), since both kinds of clause may use a Prospective *sḏm.f*, or a *sḏm.f*.

In virtual optative clauses, the translation of a Prospective *sḏm.f* into the subjunctive mood must often be left to the opinion of the translator. However, the Prospective *sḏm.f* is often used in real optative clauses, where it is introduced by a particle such as *ỉḥ* 'may'; *h3* 'would that', 'pray'; *ḥw* 'would that':

(i) *Optative clauses without introductory particle (virtual clauses)*

e.g.

ỉwt.ỉ m šms.k

may I come in your train

(alternative, non-optative, translation: I shall come in your train)

m3n.k pr n 'nḫw

may you see the house of the living

(alternatively: you will see the house of the living)

(ii) *Optative clauses with introductory particle (real clauses)*

(a) *ỉḥ*:

e.g.

ỉḥ ỉwt n.ỉ rmt

may men come to me

ỉḫ m3n.k st

may you see her

(b) 𓆎 *ḫ3*

e.g. *ḫ3 m3n.n sw*

would that we might see him

ḫ3 snbw.sn

would that they might recover

(c) *ḥw*

e.g. *ḥw ỉry.k ḫft ḏd.ỉ*

would that you would do as I say

ḥw mry.f wỉ

would that he might love me

Future tense: less common modes of expression

1. *sḏm.ỉn.f as future tense*

As we saw on page 70, the *sḏm.ỉn.f* was used to introduce an outstanding event in the *past*. It also has a function as *future tense*. Like *sḏm.ỉn.f* (past tense), *sḏm.ỉn.f* (future tense) is used only in main clauses, where it expresses the *future consequence* of an act that has already taken place; or expresses authoritative orders to perform certain actions:

e.g. If I obey the king ⟨hieroglyphs⟩

fk3.ỉn.f wỉ

then he will reward me

If you examine a man with a pain in his stomach

⟨hieroglyphs⟩

rḏỉ.ỉn.k ḏrt.k ḥr.f

then you will lay your hand upon him

In the examples quoted above, the *sḏm.f* or *sḏm.n.f* forms of the verb could have been used; but *sḏm.ỉn.f* was chosen because a more elevated form of speech was desired.

2. ⟨hieroglyphs⟩ *sḏm.ḥr.f as future tense*

The *sḏm.ḥr.f* is a verb-form that is made up in exactly the same way as the *sḏm.ỉn.f*-form (see page 70) except that the ⟨hieroglyph⟩ *ỉn* is replaced by the formative element *ḥr*.

e.g. ⟨hieroglyphs⟩   *sḏm.ḥr.ỉ*   I shall hear

⟨hieroglyphs⟩   *pr.ḥr st*   the woman will go forth

Uses of the sḏm.ḥr.f form

The *sḏm.ḥr.f* is used *only* in main clauses, with reference to future time. Like *sḏm.ỉn.f*, it can be used in statements of future consequence or to express injunctions; or as an impressive narrative tense. It is, however, less frequently used than *sḏm.ỉn.f*:

e.g. ⟨hieroglyphs⟩

st.ḥr.ỉ ḏrt.ỉ . . . I shall have to thrust my hand . . .

3. ⟨hieroglyphs⟩ *sḏm.k3.f as future tense*

The *sḏm.k3.f* is a verb form that is in structure identical with the *sḏm.ỉn.f* form (see page 70) except that ⟨hieroglyph⟩ *ỉn* is replaced by the formative element ⟨hieroglyph⟩ *k3*.

Uses of the sḏm.k3.f form

The *sḏm.k3.f* is found *only* in religious texts and temple inscriptions: it was certainly never used in spoken Middle Egyptian. It is an *emphatic* form used only in *main clauses* where it often expresses the future consequence of an act that has already taken place. In this, it resembles the way in which *sḏm.ỉn.f* is used except, of course, that *sḏm.ỉn.f* is used as an impressive narrative tense in secular stories whereas *sḏm.k3.f* is never found in a non-religious context:

e.g. [hieroglyphs]

ḥ'.k3.sn m3.sn nṯr

they shall certainly rejoice when they see the god

sḏm.ỉn.f; sḏm.ḥr.f; sḏm.k3.f—negation

There seems to have been no way to negate these verb forms, for, to date, no examples of their negation have been found in the texts.

Passive voice

All the verb forms used by the Egyptians to convey Future Tense—*sḏm.f*, Prospective *sḏm.f, sḏm.ỉn.f, sḏm.ḥr.f* and *sḏm.k3.f* (discussed above)—have passive voices formed by the insertion of the indefinite pronoun [hieroglyph] (var. [hieroglyph]) *tw* after the verb-stem, or the verb-stem plus its formative element (*ỉn, ḥr, k3*). Both the formative element and *tw* follow any determinative the verb might have; and are inseparable from the verb-stem (plus determinative, if any):

e.g. [hieroglyphs]   *dgg.tw.f*   he will be looked upon
(*sḏm.f*, passive voice)

[hieroglyphs]   *mry.tw.sn*   they will be loved
(Prospective *sḏm.f*, passive voice)

[hieroglyphs]   *ms.ỉn.tw.f*   he will be brought
(*sḏm.ỉn.f*, passive voice)

꯴꯴꯴   *sḏ.ḥr.tw.f*   it shall be removed

                                                       (*sḏm.ḥr.f*, passive voice)

꯴꯴꯴   *nḥm.k3.tw.sn*   they will be removed

                                                       (*sḏm.k3.f*, passive voice)

When the subject of any of the verb-forms listed above is a *suffix-pronoun*, it is appended directly after the *tw*. When, however, the subject is a *noun*, it may be separated from the verb and its appendages under the normal rules of word order:

e.g. ꯴꯴꯴

ꜣry.tw n.k ḥb ꜥ3

a great festival will be made for you

EXERCISE 11

(a) *Write in hieroglyphs and transliteration*

   1. His Majesty will answer the vizier, he will not answer this woman.

   2. I shall go down to the city so that I may see the temple.

   3. Then shall he be placed on his side.

   4. The god allowed her to see his face.

   5. Would that my brother would come to my house.

(b) *Translate into English*

   1. ꯴꯴꯴

   2. ꯴꯴꯴

   3. ꯴꯴꯴

   4. ꯴꯴꯴

   5. ꯴꯴꯴

Chapter 12

THE IMPERATIVE

In English, the Imperative is the form of the verb that is used to:
- (i) make commands   e.g. *Go* home!
- (ii) make requests   e.g. *Lend* me your raincoat
- (iii) entreat   e.g. *Help*!

By its very nature, the Imperative is in the 2nd person, either singular or plural. 'Go!' addressed to a single person is really 'You (sing.) go!'; addressed to a group of people it is really 'You (plural) go!'

FORMS OF THE IMPERATIVE IN MIDDLE EGYPTIAN

In Middle Egyptian, the Imperative is formed from the stem of the verb, with no distinction made as to the *gender* of the person or persons being addressed. Neither, normally, are there any special endings to denote the *singular* Imperative:

e.g. 𓄜𓏛 *sḏm* Listen!   𓏎 *ỉn* Bring! etc.,

which are written in the same way whether used as masculine or feminine singular Imperatives.

The *plural* Imperative, however, can be written with distinguishing marks. Originally, these were 𓏲 *ỉ* or, with weak verbs, 𓇌 *y*; but in Middle Egyptian, they are seldom used.

In Middle Egyptian, the *plural* Imperative *either* has *no* special ending, *or* is written with plural strokes 𓏤𓏤𓏤 , ⋮ ; and, very rarely, with a 𓅱 *w* plus plural-strokes:

e.g. 𓄜𓏛⋮ *sḏmw*; 𓄜𓏛𓅱⋮ *sḏmw*; 𓏎𓈖𓏭 *ỉnw*

N.B. The Imperatives of weak verbs *never* write out the final weak radical in transliteration:

     e.g. ỉr, Imperative of ỉrỉ 'do', 'make' (▭)

        ẖn, Imperative of ẖnỉ 'row' (▭ ▭)

Some Imperatives to note

There are two verbs which have irregular Imperatives in both singular and plural; *note* that the normal stems of both of these verbs look very different from their Imperatives:

   (i) the verb 'come'— ▭ —has the Imperatives

     (a) singular ▭ , alt. ▭ mỉ

     (b) plural ▭ my (rare)   Come!

   (ii) the verb 'give'— ▭ rdỉ —has the Imperatives

     (a) singular ▭ , alt. ▭ , ▭ etc. ỉmỉ

     (b) plural ▭ ỉmỉw   Give!

N.B. Occasionally; Imperatives are found of the verbs ỉỉ and rdỉ that have been formed from the stems of the verbs, unchanged:

     e.g. ▭ ỉỉ; and ▭ dỉ; ▭ dy; ▭ dy; ▭ rdw. Normally, however, it is the special irregular forms that are used.

USES OF THE IMPERATIVE

1. The independent use of the Imperative is the most common:

     e.g. ▭

       ỉw r pr come into the house

     ▭

       ỉs ỉn n.ỉ ỉfd go and fetch me a cloth

             (lit: go, bring to me a cloth)—two Imperatives used

2. The Imperative is often followed by a verb in the *sḏm.f* form. In such cases, the *sḏm.f* may be translated as *a second Imperative* or as *a virtual clause of purpose*:

e.g. 𓀀𓏤�* 𓏪𓂝 𓈖𓏦 𓀀𓎡 𓏤𓅓𓏏𓆑

my nṯrw ꜣr.tn mkt.f

come, ye gods (vocative) and give him protection (lit: make you his protection)—
where *my* is the irregular Imperative of *ꜣi* 'come' (see above) and *ꜣr.tn* is the 2nd
person plural of the *sḏm.f* form of the verb *ꜣri* being used as an Imperative.

or

come, ye gods, so that you may give him protection—where *ꜣr.tn* is a virtual clause
of purpose

N.B. The *sḏm.f* form can itself act as an Imperative:

e.g. 𓎼𓂋𓎼𓂓 𓉐𓂓 𓌸𓂋𓂓 �𓏏𓂓

grg.k pr.k mr.k ḥmt.k

found your house and love your wife

3. The *subject* of the Imperative is sometimes expressed in order to reinforce the meaning
of the Imperative. The subject may be:

 (i) the dependent pronoun, 2nd person:

e.g. 𓂧𓏏𓅱 𓂧𓊃𓎡

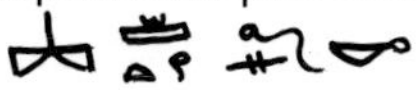

wḏ' tw ḏs.k

decide yourself (lit: give judgement you yourself)

𓄿𓀁𓏥 𓏏𓈖 𓏏𓏏𓏏

sḏmw ꜣrf tn

listen! (lit: hear you indeed yourselves)

N.B. The enclitic particle 𓏭𓂋 *ꜣrf* is often placed between the *plural* Imperative
and the dependent pronoun, for emphasis.

(ii) the suffix-pronoun, 2nd person, preceded by the preposition 𓂋 *r* (sometimes
written 𓏭𓂋 *ꜣr*):

e.g. 𓄿𓊃 𓂋𓎡 𓈖𓏭

sḏm r.k n.ꜣ

listen to me (lit: hear you to me)

𓆓𓏭𓂋𓎡 𓈖𓏭

ḏd ꜣr.k n.ꜣ

speak to me

(iii) the suffix-pronoun, 2nd person, plus the datival 〰 *n*:

e.g. 𓂝𓀀𓏤𓀁 〰 𓂋𓏤𓎛𓏤 𓅓𓊹𓏺

sḫ3 n.k hrw n ḳrs

think of the day of burial

(lit: think for yourself of the day . . .)

4. The *object* of the Imperative, when it is a pronoun, is expressed by the *dependent pronoun*:

e.g. 𓄔𓀀𓀀𓏭𓀁

m33 wỉ

look at me (lit: see thou me)

5. The Imperative of *rdỉ* (see above) followed by a verb in the *sḏm.f* form is equivalent to English 'let':

e.g. 𓇋𓂋𓃀𓈖𓇋𓃀

ỉmỉ ḏd.f ẖrt ỉb.f

let him speak his will

EXERCISE 12

(a) *Write in hieroglyphs and transliteration*

   1. Send him the despatch.
   2. Wash yourself and put water on your fingers.
   3. Come into the temple on this happy day and speak to the priest.
   4. Place (lit: give) me in your presence so that I may see your face.
   5. Let us proceed on that road.

(b) *Translate into English*

   1. 𓏺𓀀𓅓𓀁𓏭𓂋𓄤𓏤𓀁𓏤𓇋𓈖𓄿𓀁
   2. 𓃀𓏺𓈖𓃀𓏭〰𓅓𓀁𓏤𓂝𓀁𓅓
   3. 𓏺𓂋𓏤𓏤𓃀𓀁𓂝𓀁𓏤𓂝𓏤𓀁
   4. 𓉐𓀁𓈖〰𓏺𓃀𓀁𓂝𓏤𓄿〰
   5. 𓄤𓀁𓏺𓂝𓏤〰𓏤𓉐𓏤𓂝𓏤𓀁𓇳

Chapter 13

THE INFINITIVE

In English, the Infinitive of a verb simply states the action of the verb without reference to person or number; it keeps the same form whatever the subject of the verb may be.

In English, the Infinitive proper is a verb that can be employed as a noun, an adjective or an adverb:

e.g. *to go to bed* early is wise (infin. as noun, subject of 'is')

she is a girl *to be envied* (infin. as adj., describing 'girl')

she did it *to please* herself (infin. as adverb, enlarging on verb 'did' by stating reason why she did it).

It can be seen from the examples above that the verbs in their infinitive forms are prefixed by 'to', the distinguishing mark of the English Infinitive proper. In English, there are two other forms of infinitive in which the preposition 'to' is omitted; these are the *Gerunds* and the *Participles*.

Gerunds, like the Infinitive proper, are partly verbs and partly nouns:

e.g. swearing is wrong ('swearing' is a noun derived from the verb 'to swear').

The difference between the Infinitive proper and a Gerund is exemplified below, using the verbs 'carry' and 'win' as models:

Infinitive proper	*Gerund*
to carry	carrying

e.g. to carry heavy weights is arduous (Infin. proper)

carrying heavy weights is arduous (Gerund)

to win	winning

e.g. to win an Olympic medal is a great achievement (Infin. proper)

winning an Olympic medal is a great achievement (Gerund)

Participles are partly verbs, but, unlike Gerunds, they are partly adjectives instead of nouns:

e.g. the boys, *hearing* the noise, looked round ('hearing' is an adjective, describing 'boys')

Egyptian participles will be dealt with in Chapter 17.

In Egyptian, an infinitive is a *noun* formed from a verb-stem. Because it is a noun, the Egyptian Infinitive has a gender: there are masculine and feminine infinitives. The masculine infinitive has *no* distinguishing marks; the feminine infinitive ends in ⌂ *t*.

. Briefly, the following classes of verb have *feminine* infinitives:

(i) the weak verbs (i.e. those whose stems end in ⟩ *ỉ* or ⟩ *w* when written out fully in hieroglyphs):

e.g. ⟩ *prỉ* 'go forth' has Infinitive ⟩ *prt*

⟩ *ršw* 'rejoice' has Infinitive ⟩ *ršwt*

The *exceptions* to the above rule are those verbs whose stems comprise *four* radicals: e.g. ⟩ *nṯrỉ* 'be divine'. With this class of verb, some infinitives are feminine and some masculine: e.g. ⟩ *mỉnỉ* 'moor' has a masculine infinitive; but ⟩ *ḥmsỉ* 'sit down' has a feminine infinitive (⟩ *ḥmst*) (note that the *t* of the infinitive replaces the final *ỉ* in transliteration). Experience will allow the Reader to record examples of these verbs.

(ii) verbs whose stems are formed by two consonants prefixed by ⟩ *s*. By prefixing an *s* to existing words, the Egyptians could make new verbs with the meaning 'to cause to do (something)'; such verbs are called Causative Verbs:

e.g. from the verb ⟩ *mn* 'remain' comes ⟩ *smn* 'to cause to remain', 'to establish'

from the noun ⟩ *ḥb* 'festival' comes ⟩ *sḥb* 'to make festive'

In spite of ending in *strong* consonants, these Causative verbs have feminine infinitives:

e.g. ⟩ *smnt*   ⟩ *sḥbt*

Uses of the Infinitive

1. The Egyptian Infinitive often looks like one of the normal verb-forms, and, in fact, it can be used as a *narrative verb*, especially when relating events of outstanding importance:

e.g. [hieroglyphs]

n't m ḥd ỉn ḥm.f

his Majesty sailed northwards

(lit: sailing northwards (*n't*—fem. infin. of verb [hieroglyphs] *nỉ* 'travel by boat', plus preposition *m*, plus [hieroglyphs] *ḥd*, infin. of verb *ḥdỉ* 'fare downstream', which, to the Egyptians, meant travel north since the Nile flows south to north; for the construction *m* plus infin., see below page 90) by (*ỉn*) his Majesty).

N.B. The *subject* of the Infinitive (in the example above, 'his Majesty') is thought of as the agent and is therefore introduced by the preposition [hieroglyphs] *ỉn* 'by' (see page 63).

The *object* of the Infinitive, if a pronoun, is rendered by a *suffix-pronoun*. This is contrary to the rule with other parts of the verb, which is that pronominal objects are expressed by the dependent pronoun:

e.g. [hieroglyphs]

gmt.f ỉn ḥm.f

his Majesty found him

(lit: the finding (*gmt*, infin.) of him (.*f*) by his Majesty).

The reason for this use of the suffix-pronouns as objects after the Infinitive is because the Egyptians felt that the object after an Infinitive was a direct genitive after a noun; suffix-pronouns were normally employed in this capacity (see IEH, p. 80). N.B. If the object of the Infinitive is the 3rd person plural, neuter or dual, the dependent pronoun [hieroglyphs] *st* is often used in preference to a suffix-pronoun.

2. The Infinitive was often used in titles of books or in headings to ritual scenes, etc.:

e.g. [hieroglyphs]

ḥsf ꜥ3pp m wỉ3 rꜥ

to repel Apopis from the barque of Re (a magic spell)

[hieroglyphs]

ỉỉt m ḥtpw ỉn wrw nw kftyw

coming in peace by the chieftains of Crete (heading of a scene in the tomb of the Vizier, Rekhmire, Thebes, Dynasty XVIII)

𓂀𓏤𓈖𓎛   *ḏd mdw ỉn ḥwt-ḥr*

words spoken by Hathor (lit: the saying of words by Hathor)

N.B. *ḏd mdw ỉn* (a god or a king) is the formula employed at the beginning of speeches made by gods or kings inscribed on the walls of temples and tombs

3. The Infinitive can be used as the *noun subject* of a verb (equivalent of a Gerund or verbal noun in English):

e.g.   𓈖𓂧𓅓𓄖𓄖𓂋𓈖𓄖

nḏm ḫtḫt ỉm

returning (*ḫtḫt*) there is pleasant (*nḏm*)

(*ḫtḫt* is an infinitive, subject of the verb in the *sḏm.f* form, *nḏm*)

4. The Infinitive can be used as the *noun subject* in a *non-verbal sentence*:

e.g.   𓄖𓇋𓂝𓉐𓊪𓅱𓁷𓂋𓏏

nht.ỉ pw ỉrt st

it is my wish to do it (lit: my wish it is the doing of it) (the infin. (*ỉrt* 'to do') is the subject in a non-verbal sentence with nominal predicate (*nht.ỉ* 'my wish'; see page 42); the same construction can be found with non-verbal sentences with adjectival predicates).

5. The Infinitive can be used as the *object* after certain verbs: 𓌳𓂩𓂩 *m33* 'see'; 𓂋𓐍 *rh* 'know how to'; 𓇋𓎗𓏏 *wḏ* 'command'; 𓂋𓂝 *rdỉ* 'cause'; 𓄖𓂋𓂝 *3b* 'cease'; 𓄖𓂋𓄿 *3bỉ* 'desire'; 𓄖𓂩 *whm* 'repeat'; 𓄖𓅓 *mrỉ* 'love'; 𓄖𓅓 *snḏ* 'fear'; 𓄖𓂩𓂩 *sh3* 'remember'; 𓄖𓂩𓏏 *š3* 'order'; 𓄖𓂩 *š3* 'begin'; 𓂝𓂩𓅓 *k3ỉ* 'plan'

e.g.   𓌳𓂩𓂩𓈖𓄖𓂩𓂋𓏏𓎟𓈖𓏏𓍛𓆑

m33.n.ỉ š3d hrt nt hm.f

I saw to the excavation of the tomb of his Majesty

(lit: I saw the digging—*š3d*, infin. . . .)

𓂋𓐍𓂝 𓎟𓏤𓂝

rh̬.f ꜣirt st

he knows how to do it

(lit: he knows the doing (*ꜣirt*—infin.) of it

wd̲.n.ꜣ n.k ꜣirt st

I have commanded you to do it

(lit: I have commanded to you the doing (*ꜣirt*—infin.) of it)

rdꜣ.n.f n.f prt

he caused him to go forth

(lit: he gave to him the going forth (*prt*—infin.))

N.B. As we saw on page 75, the *sd̲m.f* could also be used as the object of certain verbs.

6. The Infinitive can be used *after the genitival adjective* (see IEH, p. 81):

e.g.

hrw n st tk3

the day of lighting (*st*—infin.) the lamp

This construction of genitival adjective followed by infinitive is especially common in the following cases:

(i) to express time, place, means, purpose, etc.:

e.g.

phr̲t nt sm3 hft

a remedy for (*nt*—genit. adj., fem. to agree with *phr̲t*) slaying (*sm3*—infin.) a worm

(ii) to describe how one can be, or deserves to be, treated:

e.g.

nsw swt n swhy n.f

a king indeed to be (*n*—genit. adj., masc. to agree with *nsw*) boasted (*swhy*—infin.) of

(lit: a king indeed of boasting of him).

7. The Infinitive can be used *after certain prepositions:*

(i) after ☥ *ḥr* 'upon':

e.g. 𓂝𓏤𓈖 〰 𓄿 ☥ 𓀀𓏤 𓂺

ʿ̣.n.ỉ ḥr šms.f

I returned (*ʿ̣.n.ỉ*: verb 𓂝𓏤 'return' in *sḏm.n.f* form) following (*ḥr* plus *šms*, infin.)

him (.*f*, suffix-pronoun as object of *šms*)

(lit: I returned upon the following of him)

N.B. When used after *ḥr*, the Egyptian Infinitive is often performing the same function as the English Infinitive does when it is being used to describe a noun or pronoun, that is, being used as an adjective; in other words, it is a participle (see page 125).

e.g. 𓐍𓂝𓈖𓏤𓇓𓅱𓄿☥𓉐𓂝𓏤𓉐𓂝

gm.n.f sw ḥr prt m pr.f

he found him going forth from his house

(*prt* 'going forth' is an infinitive acting as an adjective in describing *sw* 'him')

N.N.B. When used with the preposition *ḥr*, the Infinitive expresses an action that is taking place *at the same time* as the action of the verb it follows.

(ii) after 𓄿 *m* 'with':

The preposition *m* sometimes replaces *ḥr with verbs of motion.* Thus, for instance, the last example above could have been written:

𓐍𓂝𓈖𓇓𓅱𓄿𓉐𓂝𓉐𓂝

gm.n.f sw m prt m pr.f

(iii) after ◯ *r* 'to':

When used after the preposition ◯ , the Infinitive expresses *purpose* or *result:*

e.g. 𓊃𓄿𓂝𓄿◯𓏤𓏤𓄿𓏤𓏤𓂻

šm.ỉ r smỉt st

I went in order to report (*smỉt*—infin.) it

The use of the Infinitive after Prepositions led to an important development in Egyptian which will be dealt with in Chapter 15.

EXERCISE 13

(a) *Write in hieroglyphs and transliteration*

   1. My wife is nursing her little daughter.

   2. He commanded that I should go to the temple.

   3. Landing in peace by the army of the Lord of the Two Lands.

   4. A remedy for slaying a worm.

   5. It is better to give than to receive.

(b) *Translate into English*

   1.

   2.

   3.

   4.

   5.

Chapter 14

THE STATIVE

In previous chapters, the reader has become acquainted with several forms of verb, all of which come under the heading SUFFIX CONJUGATION, so called because where the subject of the verb is pronominal it is added on to the verb-stem, or to the verb-stem plus any elements which may be attached to it (e.g. ⌒𝔐 *tw*, to denote passive voice or 〰〰 *n* to denote past tense) in the form of a suffix-pronoun.

We come now to a verb-form that does *not* belong to the suffix conjugation; this verb-form is called THE STATIVE (in older grammar books it was often called the 'Old Perfective' or 'pseudo participle').

The Stative is one of the oldest verb-forms in the Egyptian language. It differs from the various forms of the suffix conjugation in that it does *not* employ suffix-pronouns to indicate pronominal subjects; instead, it has special endings of its own, which are unlike any of the Egyptian pronouns, as will be seen from the paradigm of the Stative set out below:

Singular			Plural		
1 c	⌒𝔐 ⌒ 𝔐𝔐	*sḏm.kwỉ*	1 c	⌒𝔐𝔐〰	*sḏm.wyn*
2 c	⌒𝔐𝔇𝔑 (var. ⌒𝔐⌒)	*sḏm.tỉ*	2 c	⌒𝔐𝔐〰	*sḏm.tỉwny*
		(sḏm.t(ỉ))			
3 m	⌒𝔐(𝔐)	*sḏm(w)*	3 m	⌒𝔐(𝔐)	*sḏm(w)*
3 f	⌒𝔐𝔇𝔑 (var. ⌒𝔐⌒)	*sḏm.tỉ*	3 f	⌒𝔐 𝔇𝔑	*sḏm.tỉ*, very rare; normally 3rd person plural, fem., is written as the masculine
		(sḏm.t(ỉ))			

N.B. The masculine ending 𝔐 , when written out, and the feminine ending ⌒ *t(ỉ)*, are written *before* the determinative, if any; all other endings are written after:

  e.g. 🥚𝔐𝔑 *rḫw*   🥚𝔇𝔑 *rḫ.tỉ*

As the paradigm illustrates, only the endings of the 1st singular, 1st plural and 2nd plural are at all distinctive. The 2nd singular, common, is identical with the 3rd fem. sing.; and the 3rd masc. sing. is identical with the 3rd masc. plural. Moreover, the masculine endings are often not written out. Hence it is easy to confuse the abbreviated writings ⌒𓏏𓏤 (for ⌒𓏏𓏤𓅱 *sḏm.w*) and ⌒𓏏𓏤𓂝 (for ⌒𓏏𓏤𓏏𓇋 *sḏm.tí*) with other forms of the verb. *Because of this, it is essential that the ways in which the Stative can be used should be given close attention.*

Uses of the Stative

Originally, the Stative seems to have been a multi-purpose form. It could be used in the narrative tense, past, present or future, in any person, freely, with active or passive meaning. In Middle Egyptian, however, its use became greatly restricted.

In Middle Egyptian, the tense into which the Stative is normally translated depends on context; but when it is used as a *narrative* verb, then it must be translated into the English past (heard, was heard) or present perfect (has heard, has been heard) tenses. Whether or not the Stative can be used at all depends upon three things:

(1) whether the clause in which it is to be used is Main or Subordinate;

(2) the number and person of the subject of the verb;

(3) the *type* of verb being used.

N.B. *Type of verb*

In Egyptian, as in English, verbs can be Transitive or Intransitive. *Transitive verbs* are those which can take a direct object:

e.g. 'to place' or 'to put':

John put jam on the bread

In this sentence, 'put' is the verb; 'John' is the subject (i.e. the person performing the action of the verb); 'jam' is the object (i.e. the thing receiving the action of the verb); 'put', therefore, is a *transitive verb*. ('on the bread' is an adverbial phrase telling you where John put the jam).

Intransitive Verbs are those which do *not* take a direct object:

e.g. 'to die':

> The captain died at the helm
>
> In this sentence, 'the captain' is the subject of the verb 'died'; 'at the helm' is an adverbial phrase. There is no direct object—a person can perform the action of the verb 'die', and thus be its subject; but there can be no receiver of the action of the verb—you can not say 'X died Y'; thus, there is no object to receive the action of the verb, 'die'; the action stays with the person performing it. 'Die', therefore, is an Intransitive Verb.

Some verbs can be both Transitive and Intransitive: e.g. 'kick': 'I kicked furiously'—'furiously' is an adverb describing 'kicked'; there is no object, therefore the verb is Intransitive.

'I kicked the ball'—'the ball' is the direct object of 'kicked', therefore the verb is Transitive.

Some verbs are always Intransitive: e.g. 'gape', 'default'. You can gape *at* something, default *on* a debt, but you cannot gape or default a direct object.

The most obviously Intransitive types of verb are 1) verbs of motion (go, come, travel, etc.) and 2) verbs of quality (be glad, be rich, etc.). *In Egyptian,* verbs of quality are called *Adjective Verbs.* As you would expect from the term 'adjective verb', such verbs describe something or somebody. Nearly all Egyptian adjectives have their corresponding verbs:

e.g.　　　　　*nfr* 'beautiful':

> 　　　　*ḥmt nfrt* 'a beautiful woman'
>
> 　　　　where *nfrt* is an adjective;
>
> 　　　　*nrf ḥmt* 'the woman is beautiful'
>
> 　　　　where *nfr* is the *sḏm.f* verb-form with *ḥmt* as noun subject.

N.B. According to rule, in the first example *nfr* as adjective follows its noun and agrees with it in number and gender, giving *nfrt.* In the second example, *nfr* as verb precedes its subject and remains unchanged as the verb-stem does not reflect the gender or number of its subject.

THE STATIVE IN MAIN CLAUSES

(1) In Main Clauses, the Stative 1st person (singular and plural) is used freely and independently in narrative in the following cases:

    (i) with intransitive verbs:

      e.g.

      rs.kwỉ hr.s I was watchful concerning it

      sḏr.wyn m pr.f we spent the night in his house

    N.B. The Stative of intransitive verbs lays stress on the result of the action of the verb or emphasises the state in which the subject finds himself. It could almost be translated as 'I was in a state of' e.g. the first example above—'I was in a watchful state concerning it'.

    (ii) with verbs of motion:

      e.g.

      ỉỉ.kwỉ r bw pn I came to this place

      hn.kwỉ r ỉw n w3ḏ-wr I stopped at an island of the Great Green (the sea)

    N.B. The Stative of verbs of motion, although having an *active* meaning rather than a passive, often stresses the position reached as a *result* of the movement: perhaps a better translation of the second example above would be 'I am come to this place'.

    (iii) with adjective verbs:

      e.g.

      špss.kwỉ I was rich

    N.B. The Stative of adjective verbs stresses the duration of the state described.

    (iv) with transitive verbs: passive meaning:

    when the Stative 1st person is used with transitive verbs it usually has *passive* meaning:

      e.g.

      gs-kwỉ m ḥwt-nṯr I was anointed in the temple

N.B. This narrative use of 1st person in transitive/passive verbs is often best translated in the *past* tense. If an *active* past tense is required, the *sdm.n.f* is used.

(v) with transitive verbs: active meaning:

e.g.   𓊢𓏤 ⯈ 𓄿𓏤 ⯈ 𓏤 ⯈ 𓊪𓏤 ⯈ 𓏤

wd.kwỉ rn.ỉ r bw pn I set my name at this place

N.B. The use of 1st person Stative in transitive/active verbs is rare. The exception to this rule is the verb ⬡𓏤 *rḫ* 'know'.

We have seen already (p. 66) that the Egyptians considered the verb 'know' to mean 'having learned'. It is natural, therefore, that the Stative of *rḫ* should convey the impression that a process of learning has been gone through in order to reach the state of knowing. Hence the frequent use of the 1st person Stative with the verb *rḫ*:

e.g. ⬡𓏤 ⯈ 𓄿𓏤 𓎟 ⯈ 𓊪𓏤 𓎟 ⯈ 𓏤

rḫ.kwỉ ḥtp.f m m33.f st

I knew that he would be pleased when he saw her

(2) In Main Clauses, the Stative 2nd and 3rd persons, singular and plural, are used *only* in greetings, exhortations, wishes etc., where they are in optative or imperative mood:

(i) 𓄿𓏤 𓏤 𓄿𓏤

ỉỉ.tỉ Welcome! (lit: may you be come)

Often reinforced by 𓊪𓎟 *m ḥtp* 'in peace'

e.g. 𓂧𓏤 𓏤𓏤𓏤 ⯈ 𓄿𓏤 𓊪𓎟

ḏd.sn n.f ỉỉ.tỉ m ḥtp

they said to him 'welcome!'

(ii) 𓉔𓏤𓄿𓏤 𓈖𓏤 ⯈

ḥr.tỉwny r Beware! (lit: be you far from)

Formed from the verb 𓉔𓊪 *ḥr* 'be far' plus Stative 2nd person plural written with a ⌒ plus preposition *r*

(iii) 𓋴𓄿𓄿𓏤 𓄿𓏤 𓉔

s33.tỉ ḥr Beware! (lit: guard you against/on account of)

e.g. 𓁷𓏤𓋴𓀁𓅓𓂝𓏏𓏦

ḥr.tỉwny r wnm ḥḥ n ḏ3b

Beware of eating many figs!

s33.tỉ ḥr ỉrp

Beware of wine!

(iv) 𓊪𓏲𓏏

snb.tỉ Farewell! (lit: be you healthy)

(v) 𓋹𓇰𓋴

'nḫ(w) wḏ3(w) snb(w) Life, prosperity, health!

This very common expression, which was employed, especially post Dynasty XVIII, after words referring to the King or the royal residence, is a series of 3rd person Statives. Similar expressions are: *'nḫ(w) ḏt* 'may he live forever' placed after the names of kings; and *'nḫ.tỉ* 'may she live' after the names of royal ladies.

e.g. *snb.tỉ nb.ỉ ỉỉ.k r pr-nsw 'nḫ(w) wḏ3(w) snb(w)*
m ḥtp

Farewell, my lord. May you return to the Palace (life, prosperity, health!—often abbreviated to l.p.h.) in safety.

THE STATIVE IN SUBORDINATE CLAUSES

It can be seen from the examples of the use of the Stative in Main Clauses that the overriding feeling of the Stative is one of passivity: hence the term 'Stative' for a verb-form that describes the state its subject finds him/her/itself in.

Not surprisingly, then, the Stative is used much more frequently in subordinate clauses than in main clauses; and, whereas in main clauses the use of 2nd and 3rd person Stative is restricted, in subordinate clauses *all* persons are used.

In subordinate clauses, the Stative marks a state, a condition, the *result* of an action (*not* the action itself). The subordinate clause is often a *virtual clause of circumstance* (i.e. a clause of time, place or manner which in English is introduced by 'while', 'as', 'where', etc.) or a *virtual relative clause* (introduced by 'which', 'who', etc.; see page 120); and in fact the use of the Stative as a virtual clause of circumstance is its chief use.

N.B. The Stative in the subordinate clause *must link up* with a noun or pronoun in the main clause; the Stative then describes or qualifies this noun or pronoun in some way:

e.g. He found him lying down

gm.n.f sw sḏr(w)

Main clause: *gm.n.f sw*—verb (*gmỉ*—find) in *sḏm.n.f*-form with pronoun subject (*f*); object *sw* (dependent pronoun): he found him;

subordinate clause: *sḏr(w)* (lying down): 3rd person Stative, masculine singular, describing *sw* in main clause.

She came to him as he was standing there

ỉỉ.n.s. n.f ꜥḥꜥ(w) ỉm

Main clause: *ỉỉ.n.s n.f*—verb (*ỉỉ*—come) in *sḏm.n.f*-form with pronoun subject (*s*); 'to come to somebody' is verb *ỉỉ* plus preposition ~~~ *n*—*n.f.* 'to him': she came to him;

subordinate clause: *ꜥḥꜥ(w) ỉm*—*ỉm* is an adverb (there); *ꜥḥꜥ(w)* 'standing' is Stative 3rd person masculine in a virtual clause of circumstance, picking up the indirect object in the main clause (*f*) 'him' and describing the circumstance 'he' was in, i.e. standing there.

He saw a woman who was pregnant

m3.n.f ḥmt ỉwr.tỉ

Main clause: *m3.n.f ḥmt* (he saw a woman);

subordinate clause: *ỉwr.tỉ* (who was pregnant), a virtual relative clause with the Stative in the 3rd person singular, feminine, qualifying 'woman' in the main clause.

EXERCISE 14

(a) *Write in hieroglyphs and transliteration*

1. She is the wife of a priest of Re who is pregnant with three children.
2. The king came in a chariot wrought with gold.
3. He found the priest seated in the temple.
4. I was placed in the house of a king's son.
5. There is said to him 'welcome' by all the gods.

(b) *Translate into English*

1.
2.
3.
4.
5.

Chapter 15

THE PSEUDO-VERBAL CONSTRUCTION

The term 'Pseudo-verbal Construction' is applied to sentences in which either a Stative or a preposition plus Infinitive (usually the preposition is ḥr, less frequently m or r, see below p. 103) serves as *predicate* (see p. 41) to a preceding noun or pronoun *in either* main *or* subordinate clauses.

The predicate in such cases is considered to be *adverbial*. This is obviously the case with the construction ḥr (or m or r) plus Infinitive because a preposition plus a noun (the Infinitive is, of course, a noun, see p.86) is the way in which an adverbial phrase is made up in Egyptian. It is not so obvious that the Stative is adverbial; however, the fact that the Stative in Middle Egyptian was chiefly used in subordinate clauses led to it being regarded as a virtual adverbial clause, so that in the Pseudo-verbal Construction the Stative, like the Infinitive, is used as an adverbial predicate.

In the Pseudo-verbal Construction, preposition plus Infinitive normally expresses an action or an event, whereas the Stative marks a state, the result of an action. *Tense* often depends upon context, but the Stative tends to mark the past, ḥr plus Infinitive the present (as does m plus Infinitive), r plus Infinitive the future.

1. Pseudo-verbal Construction with noun subject

(i) If the *subject* of a Pseudo-verbal sentence is a *noun*, it can stand alone at the beginning of the sentence:

e.g.

ḥ3tt rdỉ.t(ỉ) ḥr t3 . . . s nb ḥr ḥpt snnw.f

the prow-rope is placed on shore . . . every man embraces his mate

[Stative (rdỉ.t(ỉ)) and ḥr plus Infinitive (ḥr ḥpt) in parallelism]

(ii) However, a noun subject is often introduced by particles such as 𓀁 𓂺 *mk*, 𓇋𓈖𓂝 *ꜣst*, etc.:

e.g. 𓀁𓂺 𓅡 𓈖𓂝𓄔 𓂻𓀎

  mt sꜣ-nht ꜣw

  lo, Sinuhe is returned

    [Stative (*ꜣw*)]

  𓇋𓈖𓂝 𓁷 𓂋 𓆓𓂧

  ꜣst hm.f hr dd

  lo, His Majesty is speaking

    [*hr* plus Infinitive (*dd*)]

(iii) If a *noun* subject is preceded by the verb 𓇋𓅱 *ꜣw* (see p. 107) then it is part of a *main* clause, normally with past or present meaning:

e.g. 𓇋𓅱𓊹𓊪 𓂺 𓄿𓏏 𓅓 �htp

  ꜣw ntr pn wdꜣ(w) m htp

  this God proceeded in peace

    [Stative (*wdꜣ(w)*)]

  𓇋𓅱𓆷𓂝 𓂺 𓆓 𓄿𓄿

  ꜣw mšꜥ pn hr mꜣꜣ

  this army looked on

    [*hr* plus Infinitive (*mꜣꜣ*)]

(iv) If a noun subject is preceded by the verb 𓃂 *wn* (see p. 109) then it is part of a *subordinate* clause; *wn* in its turn can be introduced by a preposition or conjunction:

e.g. I have done this 𓈖 𓌸𓂋𓅱𓏏 𓃂 𓂋𓈖 𓏇𓈖

    n-mrwt wn rn.ꜣ mn(w)

    in order that my name might be established

      [Stative (*mn(w)*)]

  You shall do this 𓂋 𓃂 𓎟𓎡 𓁷 𓎛𓋴𓏏𓎡

    r wn nb.k hr hst.k

    so that your master may praise you

      [*hr* plus Infinitive (*hst*)]

2. Pseudo-verbal Construction with pronoun subject

(i) When the subject of a Pseudo-verbal sentence is a pronoun, the dependent pronouns are normally used. These, as we have learned, can not stand alone at the beginning of a sentence: they must have some other word to lean on; and in the Pseudo-verbal Construction, that word is often a particle such as 🐦 *mk*, 🐦 *ꜣst*, etc.:

e.g. 🐦 *mk wꜣ ꜣꜣ.kwꜣ*

behold, I have come (*or* am come)

(lit: behold me, I am come)

    [Stative (*ꜣꜣ.kwꜣ*)]

🐦 *ꜣst sw ḥr ḏd*

lo, he is speaking

(lit: lo/behold him upon speaking)

    [*ḥr* plus Infinitive (*ḏd*)]

(ii) Sometimes, a suffix-pronoun is used as the subject of a Pseudo-verbal sentence. A suffix-pronoun subject, like a noun subject, can be introduced by 🐦 *ꜣw* (see above, 1 (iii)). However, in the case of the suffix-pronoun subject, this need *not* necessarily indicate a main clause: the suffix-pronoun, by definition, must have something to be affixed to:

e.g. 🐦 *ꜣw.f sspd m bw nb nfr*

it is prepared with every good thing

    [*ꜣw* plus suffix *f* plus Stative (*sspd*) in main clause]

but

🐦 *sḏm.n.ꜣ ḥrw.f ꜣw.f ḥr mdt*

I heard his voice as he was speaking

    [*ꜣw* plus suffix *f* plus *ḥr* plus Infinitive (*mdt*) in subordinate clause]

(iii) A suffix-pronoun subject may also lean on the verb 𓄿𓏏 *wn* (with or without an introductory preposition or conjunction), in which case, *wn* introduces a *subordinate* clause:

e.g. 𓂧𓏤𓈖𓀁𓇋𓏏𓄿𓆑𓂋𓅱

ḏd n.ỉ ỉt.ỉ wn.f mr(w)

my father spoke to me when he was ill

    [*wn.f* plus Stative (*mr(w)*)]

You shall do this

𓄿𓏏𓏤𓎛𓀁𓊪𓏏𓂝

wn.f ḥr ḥst.k

so that he shall praise you

    [*wn.f* plus *ḥr* plus Infinitive (*ḥst*)]

3. Substitutes for 𓎛𓏤 *ḥr*

Although the preposition most commonly used with the Infinitive in the Pseudo-verbal Construction is *ḥr*, it is often replaced by 𓅓 *m* or 𓂋 *r* in the following instances:

(i) *m* replaces *ḥr* before verbs of motion, apparently in order to stress the durative character of the action:

e.g. 𓆑𓅓𓈖𓏤𓆑𓅱𓉐𓏤𓇋𓅱𓆑𓅓𓇌𓏏

gm.n.ỉ ḥf3w pw ỉw.f m ỉỉt

I found it was a serpent that was coming

    (lit: it was in coming)

I conducted the King

𓇋𓅱𓆑𓅓𓌢𓈖𓏤𓂋𓎡𓈅

ỉw.f m ḫntyt r K3s

    when he was sailing upstream to Kush

    or as he sailed upstream to Kush

(ii) *r* replaces *ḥr* in order to stress *futurity*:

e.g. 𓄣𓈖𓎛𓅓𓎡𓂋𓎡𓃀𓃀𓈗

ỉb n ḥm.k r kbb

the heart of your Majesty will be refreshed

mk wỉ r nḥm '3.k

behold, I will take away your ass

ỉw.f r ỉtt t3w rsyw

he will seize the southern lands

N.B. The various ways of introducing the subject found with *ḥr* plus Infinitive repeat themselves with *m* and *r*. Particularly common is *ỉw.f r sdm* (see above, 2 (ii), for examples using *ḥr*), which survived into Coptic as a Future Tense ЄЧЄ СⲰⲦⲘ (ef-ay-so-tem) 'he will hear'.

4. Pseudo-verbal Construction with auxiliary verbs

See Chapter 16.

5. Negation of the Pseudo-verbal Construction

The Pseudo-verbal Construction seems to have been negated very rarely indeed. The Egyptians, if they wished to negate an action that could be considered to be continuous or repeated preferred to use *n sdm.n.f* (see IEH, p. 105). If they wished to negate an action taking place in the future, they used *nn sdm.f* (see IEH. p. 105).

6. The choice between ḥr plus Infinitive and the Stative

The beginner often finds the differences in meaning between *ḥr* plus Infinitive and the Stative difficult to comprehend. This does not matter so much in translating from English into Egyptian which is, after all, an academic exercise. It is important, however, when translating from Egyptian into English; otherwise, significant nuances may be lost.

Take, for example, the name of one of Egypt's most famous queens, Nefertiti. It is

ḥr plus Infinitive	Stative
(i) with transitive verbs: active, stresses action: *ḥmt.f ḥr m33.ỉ* his wife is looking at me	(i) with transitive verbs: passive, ***stresses result: *ḥmt.f m33.tỉ ỉn.ỉ* his wife is seen by me
(ii) with intransitive verbs: describes the event: *s ḥr mwt* the man is dying	(ii) with intransitive verbs: describes state after event: *ỉw.s mwt.tỉ* she was/is dead
(iii) with verbs of motion: stresses the movement itself: *ỉw.s m ỉỉt* she is coming	(iii) with verbs of motion: stresses result of movement: *mk sy ỉỉ.tỉ* behold, she is come
(iv) with adjective verbs: rare, stresses the process of becoming: *ỉtn ḥr m3w(y)* the sun's disk is new i.e. renews itself	(iv) with adjective verbs: very common, stresses state of being: *kmt nfr.tỉ* Egypt is happy
	*** The verbs *rḫ* (know) and *ḏd* (say) are exceptions; they are often used with *active* meaning in the Stative

generally agreed that *nefert* means 'the beautiful woman' and that 𓏠 should, more correctly, be written 𓏠.𓏏 i.e. 3rd person feminine Stative of the verb 𓏠 'come'. The name is often translated as 'The beautiful woman *has* come', which misses the nuance of the Stative. If, however, Nefertiti is translated as 'The beautiful woman *is* come', this rendering gives greater importance to the act of coming, suggesting that her coming was an event awaited with great expectancy.

An inadvertent use of a Stative came during the Coronation of Queen Elizabeth II when the commentator for the BBC broadcast, Richard Dimbleby, chose to say when the Queen was about to be crowned, 'The moment of crowning is come' and *not* 'The moment of crowning has come'. This choice of words aroused some comment at the time, but 'is come' conveyed the same sense of an eagerly awaited event that Nerfertiti's name does.

To sum up: in the Pseudo-verbal Construction, *ḥr* plus Infinitive describes an act or event and is *active*; the Stative describes a condition or the result of an action and is passive in feeling—not necessarily, however, a passive *tense*. The differences in meaning between the two are illustrated in the table on page 105:

EXERCISE 15

(a) *Write in hieroglyphs and transliteration*
   1. Then a ship will come from Egypt.
   2. I cast myself upon my belly, my arms folded in his presence.
   3. Behold, you will arrive in Egypt in two months.
   4. Behold, I am coming to sit in this house.
   5. His Majesty sailed southwards, his heart rejoicing.

(b) *Translate into English*
   1.
   2.
   3.
   4.
   5.

Chapter 16

AUXILIARY VERBS

In English, auxiliary verbs are those that are used in conjunction with other verbs to help form some of the tenses of the other verbs:

e.g. 'she has gone'—a past tense formed from the verbs 'have' and 'go'; 'I do like cake'— an emphatic tense formed from the verbs 'do' and 'like'.

The chief auxiliary, or helping, verbs in English are to be, to have, to do.

In Egyptian, the various forms of suffix-conjugation, and, to a lesser extent, the Pseudo-verbal Construction, have one feature in common: *imprecision* regarding *tense*. The *sḏm.f*, in particular, can be past, present or future, although matters are improved in the Pseudo-verbal Construction where, for example, *r* plus Infinitive is definitely future tense.

As far back as the Old Kingdom, the suffix-conjugation was often replaced by tenses based on the Pseudo-verbal Construction. Gradually, the Egyptians evolved a method, or rather, methods, whereby they could be much more precise about tense. However, by the time they had devised methods of indicating tenses which mark distinctions of time as precisely as, say, English or French, Egyptian had become Coptic!

The process seems to have begun with the use of the verb 𓇌𓏭 *ꞽw* 'come' as an auxiliary verb introducing the *sḏm.f* or *sḏm.n.f* forms to give them shades of meaning (see p. 67). The Egyptians later supplemented *ꞽw* by two other auxiliary verbs, 𓃹𓈖𓈖 *wnn* 'exist' and 𓊢𓂝 *ꜥḥꜥ* 'stand up'. Thus, in Middle Egyptian, the chief auxiliary verbs are *ꞽw, wnn* and *ꜥḥꜥ*: and all of these verbs, when used as auxiliaries, can have nominal or pronominal subjects. When pronominal, the subject is expressed by the suffix-pronouns. All three verbs also have an independent life of their own, and can be used as verbs with their original meanings of 'come', 'exist' and 'stand up' respectively.

1. 𓇌𓏭 *ꞽw*: when used as an auxiliary verb, *ꞽw* probably means something like 'the situation is' e.g. *ꞽw sḏm.f* 'the situation is he hears'. *ꞽw* is left untranslated, however, so

that the example just given would simply be rendered as 'he hears'. It is used in the following constructions:

(i) 𓄿𓆑 𓂋𓊃𓂋 *ỉw sḏm.f*: this construction is particularly common in past narrative, or to describe a prolonged state of affairs:

e.g. 𓄿𓆑 𓂝𓆑 𓈖 𓈖𓆓𓋴

ỉw ỉr.ỉ n nḏs

I acted on behalf of the poor man

(lit: the situation is I acted for the poor man)

𓄿𓆑 𓎛𓅓𓊃 𓏏𓅱 𓁷 𓂧𓅓𓏭

ỉw ḥms tw ḥr dmỉ

One (i.e. the King) was besieging a city

(ii) 𓄿𓆑 𓂋𓊃𓏏𓅱𓆑 *ỉw sḏm.tw.f*: this construction is frequently used in generalizations, and is, of course, passive:

e.g. 𓄿𓆑 𓂞𓏏𓅱 𓈖𓆑 𓏏 𓎛𓈖𓎡𓏏

ỉw dỉ.tw n.f t ḥnkt

Bread and beer are given to him

(iii) 𓄿𓆑 𓂋𓊃𓆑 *ỉw.f sḏm.f*: in this construction, the subject, be it noun or pronoun, is attached to the auxiliary verb *and also* to the following *sḏm.f* form of the verb:

e.g. 𓄿𓆑 𓈖𓆓𓅓𓆑

ỉw.f nḏm.f he will get well

𓄿𓆑 𓂋 𓈖 𓊃 𓈖𓎛𓅓𓆑 𓇋𓅱

ỉw r n s nḥm.f sw

a man's mouth saves him

(lit: it is the situation that the mouth of a man it saves him)

The meaning and uses of the *ỉw.f sḏm.f* form are practically identical with those of *ỉw sḏm.f*. It should be noted, however, that it can be used as a virtual subordinate clause:

e.g. 𓂋𓊃𓈖𓏭 𓏌𓂋𓅱𓆑 𓄿𓆑 𓅓𓂧𓅱𓆑

sḏm.n.ỉ ḥrw.f ỉw.f mdw.f

I heard his voice as he was speaking (virtual clause of time)

(iv) 𓀀𓄿𓆑𓏏𓏤 *ꞽw sḏm.n.f*: this very common narrative past tense is used to introduce events of some importance. It has already been discussed in the section on past tense (see p. 67).

(v) *ꞽw* plus passive *sḏm.f*: the *sḏm.n.f* past tense, active voice, is paralleled by the passive *sḏm.f* past tense, passive voice (see p. 69). The construction *ꞽw* plus passive *sḏm.f* is found *only when the subject is a noun*; there seem to be no examples with a pronominal subject:

e.g. 𓀀𓄿𓂝𓄿𓏤𓏲𓄿

ꞽw rdꞽw n.k ṯꜣw

breath has been given to you

N.B. Impersonal uses are frequent with *ꞽw* plus passive *sḏm.f*:

e.g. 𓀀𓄿𓂋𓏭𓂝𓄿𓆑

ꞽw ꞽr mꞽ ḏd.f

it was done as he said

(vi) 𓀀𓄿 was also used in the Pseudo-verbal Construction (see p. 101). In this construction, *ꞽw* with noun subject marks a main clause; *ꞽw* with pronoun subject can introduce either a main or a subordinate clause.

2. 𓃹𓈖 *wnn* (sometimes written 𓃹 or 𓈖 *wn*): the geminating and non-geminating forms of 𓃹 (to exist) are normally used in conjunction with the elements 𓈖 *ꞽn* and 𓁷 *ḥr* to make up the auxiliary verbs *wn.ꞽn, wn.ḥr* and *wnn.ḥr*; they are most often found in the following constructions:

(i) 𓃹𓈖 *wn.ꞽn.f* plus the Pseudo-verbal Construction was a common method of writing the past narrative tense:

e.g. 𓈖𓏤𓀀𓁷𓄿𓃀𓏤𓂝𓂡

wn.ꞽn ḥm.f ḥr ḥꜣk.s

then His Majesty captured it

(*wn.ꞽn.f* with noun subject (*ḥm.f*) plus *ḥr* plus Infinitive (*ḥꜣk*))

𓃹𓈖𓀀𓊪𓏏𓄑𓂝𓏤𓅓𓂝𓄿𓏤𓂡

wn.ꞽn.ꞽ ptḫ.kwꞽ m-bꜣḥ.f

then I lay prostrate before him

(*wn.ꞽn.f* with pronoun subject (*ꞽ*) plus Stative (*ptḫ.kwꞽ*))

(ii) 𓂝𓈖𓎡𓆰 *wn.ḥr.f* was often used in the Pseudo-verbal Construction, where it normally denoted the *past* tense:

e.g. 𓂝𓈖𓎡𓆰𓏲𓂝𓏤𓆼𓈖𓏏𓏲𓏛𓂻

wn.ḥr.ỉ ḥr ḳnt ḥr rdwy.ỉ

then I displayed valour upon my feet

(*wn.ḥr.f* with pronoun subject (*ỉ*) plus *ḥr* plus Infinitive (*ḳnt*)

𓂝𓈖𓎡𓎛𓋴𓅱𓏏𓈖𓏏𓏭

wn.ḥr ḥswt.ỉ mn.tỉ

then my praises were established

(*wn.ḥr.f* with noun subject (*ḥswt*) plus Stative (*mn.tỉ*)

(iii) 𓂝𓈖𓈖𓆰 *wnn.ḥr.f* was also used in the Pseudo-verbal Construction, although much less often than *wn.ḥr.f*; but where it was used, it denoted the *future* tense. This might be considered superfluous, since the Construction had a way of indicating future tense using *r* plus Infinitive (see p. 103). However, the use of *wnn.ḥr.f* plus *Stative* in the Pseudo-verbal Construction enabled the Stative, which was by its nature more suited to be a past tense, to be more precisely defined, where necessary, as a future tense:

e.g. 𓂝𓈖𓈖𓅱𓂋𓏤𓎡𓅓𓈙𓂝𓏏𓆱𓂻

wnn.ḥr s nb ḥr ỉrt pḥty

then shall every man display valour

(*wnn.ḥr.f* with noun subject (*s*) plus *ḥr* plus Infinitive (*ỉrt*)

𓂝𓈖𓈖𓅱𓂝𓏏𓅓𓂝𓈖𓈖𓆑𓏏𓊪𓏤𓇾

wnn.ḥr.f w3ḏ mỉ wnn.f tp t3

then shall he be flourishing as he was upon earth (*wnn.ḥr.f* with pronoun subject (*f*) plus Stative (*w3ḏ*)

N.B. *wnn.ḥr.f* plus Stative can mark not only a future tense but also the *duration* of a state (as in first example above).

3. 𓊽𓂝𓂻 *ʿḥʿ*: the verb *ʿḥʿ*, which means 'stand up' or 'arise', was used as an auxiliary verb *in main clauses only*. It was most often used in its *sḏm.n.f* form as an auxiliary verb to a following *sḏm.n.f*, both verbs having the same subject; and *ʿḥʿ.n sḏm.n.f* must originally have meant something like '(he) stood up and he heard'. Gradually,

however,the *'ḥ'* lost its literal significance: and when translating *'ḥ.n sdm.n.f* it is not necessary to render it 'he stood up etc', but simply as 'he heard'. When used as an auxiliary verb, *'ḥ'* is often written without its determinative ⌐. The most common constructions using *'ḥ'* as auxiliary verb are:

(i) 𒀭𒀭𒀭𒀭 *'ḥ.n sdm.n.f.* As was stated above, in this construction *'ḥ'* is in the *sdm.n.f* form, taking the same subject as the verb to which it is acting as auxiliary, although in the case of *'ḥ'* itself it is unneccessary to express the subject. *'ḥ.n sdm.n.f* is a very common narrative tense and was used normally to introduce incidents of outstanding interest:

e.g. 𒀭𒀭𒀭𒀭

'ḥ.n wšb.n.s n.f

then she answered him

𒀭𒀭𒀭𒀭

'ḥ.n ỉn.n w'w skḥ-'nḥ

then the soldier brought in a living captive

(ii) 𒀭𒀭 *'ḥ.n* plus passive *sdm.f*. The passive of the construction in paragraph (i) above is formed by placing the passive *sdm.f* form of a verb after the *'ḥ.n*. The construction *'ḥ.n* plus passive *sdm.f* was used most frequently with noun subjects, or impersonally; pronoun subjects were not common:

e.g. 𒀭𒀭𒀭𒀭

'ḥ.n sspd 'ḥ'w n s3-nsw ḥrddf

thereupon ships were made ready for Prince Hardedef

(passive *sdm.f* – *'ḥ'w* – with noun subject – *'ḥ'w*)

𒀭𒀭𒀭𒀭

'ḥ.n ỉrw mỉ dd.n.f

then it was done according to what he had said

(passive *sdm.f* – *ỉrw* – used impersonally)

(iii) 𒀭𒀭 *'ḥ.n.f* plus Pseudo-verbal Construction:

(a) *'ḥ.n.f* plus *ḥr* plus Infinitive: this construction was not common since *'ḥ.n. sdm.n.f* (see 3 (i) above) covered the same ground. *Note that the subject of the verb is attached to the auxiliary '*ḥ*': ḥr plus Infinitive must have the subject* of the sentence, whether noun or pronoun, expressed *before* ḥr:

e.g. [hieroglyphs]

'ḥ'.n.tw ḥr ỉw'.ỉ m nbw

then One rewarded me with gold

N.B. Very occasionally, the particle [hieroglyphs] mk

(alt. [hieroglyphs]) replaces ḥr in this construction:

e.g. [hieroglyphs]

'ḥ'.n.tw mk ỉw'.ỉ m nbw ḥr sn-nw.sy

then One rewarded me with gold yet again

(b) 'ḥ'.n.f plus Stative: this construction was commonly used with verbs of motion and with verbs expressing a state or condition, when the Stative describes an event or an action. As with ḥr plus Infinitive (see section (iii) (a) above) the *subject* must be expressed *before* the Stative; and, in the case of the Stative, picked up again and expressed *in* the Stative:

e.g. [hieroglyphs]

'ḥ'.n.ỉ šm.kwỉ ḥn'.f

then I went with him

[hieroglyphs]

'ḥ'.n dpt m(w)t.t(ỉ)

then the ship perished

AUXILIARY VERBS: ADDITIONAL NOTE

It can be seen from the examples given in this Chapter that it is difficult to translate auxiliary verbs in their various constructions into English; the translator often falls back upon the rather lame 'then he did something'. We must presume that to the Egyptians themselves these constructions using auxiliary verbs imparted varying degrees of liveliness, importance and excitement. Many of the stories in which they are found would, of course, have been spoken aloud for the benefit of an enthralled audience by a storyteller, since the majority of Egyptians were illiterate; and in such stories, the auxiliary constructions are often used in a seemingly monotonous and repetitive way. However, as many of us know from telling stories to children, repetition and 'catch phrases' are essential in a story heard rather than read. For example, in the Tale of Goldilocks and the Three Bears, the refrain 'one for the father bear, one for the mother bear and one for the baby bear' applied in turn to plates, cups, chairs and beds, is a key part of the story. So must repetition have been important in Egyptian stories. It is, therefore, a challenge for the translator to find a way to distinguish between auxiliary constructions and to render them in a lively way!

EXERCISE 16

The time has come for the reader to attempt a translation of a continuous piece of Egyptian prose. The excerpt below is taken from the biography of a naval officer, Ahmose, who served under three successive kings of Dynasty XVIII—Ahmose I, Amenhotep I and Tuthmosis I. The biography is inscribed on two walls in Ahmose's tomb at El-Kab in Upper Egypt.

   In order to help the reader with his translation, a transliteration has been provided; and some philological notes are appended after the text which refer the reader to relevant sections in the Grammar. Points to note: the capital city of the Hyksos was called *ḥwt-w'rt*—the Mansion of the Leg, later called Avaris; Avaris was approached by a canal called *ḏdkw; ḫ'-m-mn-nfr* ('Shining in Memphis') was the name of Ahmose's ship; 𓇋 = 𓃀 ; 𓐠 = 𓈖 ; 𓂋 = 𓃭 .

The war against the Hyksos

1. *wn.ḥr.ỉ   ḥr šms   ỉty   'nḥ wḏꜣ snb   ḥr rdwy.ỉ m-ḫt swtwt.f*

2. *ḥr wrr(y)t.f   ỉw ḥms.tw   ḥr dmỉ   n ḥwt-w'rt*

3. *wn.ḥr.ỉ ḥr knt   ḥr rdwy.ỉ   m-b3ḥ ḥm.f   'ḥ'.n.ỉ dhn.*

4. *kwỉ   r ḫ'-m-mn-nfr   wn.ỉn.tw   ḥr 'ḥ3   ḥr mw m*

5. *p3 ḏdkw   n ḥwt-w'rt   'ḥ'.n ḥf.n.ỉ   ỉn.ỉ*

6. *drt   smỉ.t(w) n wḥmw-nsw   wn.ỉn.tw   ḥr rdỉt n.ỉ   nbw n knt*

7. *'ḥ'.n wḥmw 'ḥ3   m st tn   wn.ỉn.ỉ   ḥr wḥm ḥf'   ỉm*

8. *ỉn. ỉ drt   wn.ỉn.tw   ḥr rdỉt n.ỉ nbw n knt   m wḥm-'   wn.ỉn.tw*

9. *ḥr 'ḥ3   m t3   kmt   rsyt n dmỉ   pn   'ḥ'.n ỉn.n.ỉ*

10. *skrỉ-'nḥ   s 1   h3.n.ỉ   r p3 mw   mk   ỉntw.f*

11. *m m mḥ   ḥr t3 w3t   p3 dmỉ   ḏ3.n.ỉ   ḥr.f   ḥr mw*

12. *smỉw   n wḥmw-nsw   'ḥ'.n.tw   mk   ỉw'.ỉ   m nbw ḥr snnw.sy*

13. *wn.ỉn.tw ḥr h3k   ḥwt-w'rt   wn.ỉn.ỉ   ḥr ỉnt   h3kwt ỉm*

14. *s 1   st-ḥmt 3   dmḏ r tp 4*

Philological notes

line 1: *wn.ḥr.ỉ*—auxiliary verb *wn ḥr* (see p. 110) in pseudo-verbal construction, i.e. followed by *ḥr* plus infinitive (*šms*) in past narrative; *'nḫ wḏ3 snb*—stative, 3rd person sing. in optative mood (see p. 96); *rdwy.ỉ*—dual noun (see IEH p. 76); *m-*

ḫt—compound preposition (see p. 3) used to introduce a following *sdm.f* form (in this case, *swtwt.f*) in a real clause of circumstance (see p. 60).

line 2: *ꞌw ḥms.tw*—auxiliary verb *ꞌw* followed by *sdm.f* in past narrative (see p. 108); *tw*—indefinite pronoun used impersonally (see pp. 27, 62), here 'One' refers to the king; verb *ḥms*, followed by prep. *ḥr* means 'to besiege'.

line 3: *wn.ḥr.ꞌ* etc.—see note on line 1 above; *m-b3ḥ*—compound preposition (see p. 3); *ꞌḥꞌ.n.ꞌ*—auxiliary verb *ꞌḥꞌ* (see p. 110) followed by stative 1st person sing. (see p. 112).

line 4: *wn.ꞌn.tw*—auxiliary verb *wn.ꞌn* (see p. 109) in pseudo-verbal construction, i.e. followed by *ḥr* plus infinitive (*ꞌḥ3*) in past narrative; *tw* again refers to king (see note on line 2 above).

line 5: *p3*—demonstrative adjective (see p. 19); *ꞌḥꞌ.n*—auxiliary verb *ꞌḥꞌ* in *sdm.n.f* form (see p. 111) followed by verb *ḥfꞌ* in *sdm.n.f* form in past narrative tense; *ꞌn.ꞌ*—*sdm.f* in past tense of verb 𓈖𓈖𓈖 *ꞌnꞌ*.

line 6: *smꞌ.t(w)*—impersonal use of indefinite pronoun (see p. 26) as subject of verb (*smꞌ*) in *sdm.f* form; *wn.ꞌn.tw*—see note on line 4 above; *n.ꞌ*—dative plus 1st person suffix-pronoun.

line 7: *ꞌḥꞌ.n*—auxiliary verb *ꞌḥꞌ* (see p. 111) followed by verb *wḥmw* (to repeat) in passive *sdm.f* form, subject *ꞌḥ3*—infinitive acting as noun, *wn.ꞌn.ꞌ ḥr wḥm*—see note on line 4 above; *wḥm* is verb meaning 'to repeat an action', the action in this case being *ḥfꞌ* 'make a capture'; *ꞌm*—adverb (see p. 1).

line 8: *ꞌn.ꞌ*—*sdm.f* in past tense of verb 𓈖𓈖𓈖 *ꞌnꞌ* (see above, line 5); *wn.ꞌn.tw* (beginning and end of line)—see note on line 4 above; *m wḥm-ꞌ*—adverbial phrase (see IEH, p. 86)

line 9: *t3*—demonstrative adjective (see p. 19); *ꞌḥꞌ.n* etc.—see note on line 5 above.

line 10: *p3*—demonstrative adjective (see p. 19); *h3.n.ꞌ*—*sdm.n.f* form with suffix-pronoun (*ꞌ*) as subject, introducing pseudo-verbal construction *mk ꞌntw.f*— 𓂝𓏏 *mk* is rare substitute for the more usual 𓁷 *ḥr*, *ꞌntw* is infinitive, with a seemingly intrusive 𓃭 *w* which is there, however, to indicate that the 𓏏 *t* is pronounced before the suffix-pronoun object *.f*.

line 11: *t3*—demonstrative adjective (see p. 19).

line 12: *'ḥ'.n.tw mk ỉw'.ỉ—sḏm.n.f* form with indefinite pronoun *tw* as subject; *mk* again substitute for *ḥr;ỉw'.ỉ*—infinitive plus suffix-pronoun object; *ḥr-snnw.sy*—adverbial phrase made up of preposition *ḥr* plus ordinal number *snnw* plus dependent pronoun *sy,* lit: 'for its second (time)', i.e. 'again'.

line 13: *wn.ỉn.tw ḥr ḥ3k*—see note to line 4 above; *wn.ỉn.ỉ ḥr ỉnt*—compare example in line 10 (see above) where the infinitive *ỉnt* has a suffix-pronoun as object: in this example, there is a *noun* object (*ḥ3kwt*), and there is therefore no need for a *w* to be written.

Chapter 17

RELATIVE CLAUSES

As we saw in Chapter 8, a sentence may be made up of several clauses, one of which is the main clause, and the other(s) a dependent clause. In a sentence, the dependent clause may play the part of a noun, an adverb or an adjective.

A dependent clause playing the part of an *adjective* is known as an adjectival clause, and, as might be expected, it *describes a noun in the main clause*. In both English and Egyptian such clauses are called *Relative Clauses*.

In *English*, relative clauses are dependent adjectival clauses which qualify a noun subject or noun object in the main clause and are linked to that clause by one of the following:

(i) a relative pronoun (who, which, what, that, as) *or*

(ii) a relative adverb (where, when, why, whence, whither):

e.g. this is the man *who built the house*

this is the house *that Jack built*

(words in italic are clauses introduced by a relative pronoun)

this is the place *where she saw him*

now is the time *when you should do it*

(words in italic are clauses introduced by a relative adverb).

In *Egyptian* also, relative clauses are dependent clauses which qualify a noun in the main clause; but *there are no relative pronouns in Egyptian*. Instead, Egyptian employs a variety of different ways of introducing a relative clause.

Relative Clauses in Egyptian

There are two types of relative clause in Egyptian:

(1) virtual relative clauses

(2) real relative clauses.

A virtual relative clause has *no* special word or verb-form to introduce it; a real relative clause is introduced by special words such as the relative adjective, or by special forms of the verb such as the relative form (see below, pp. 120, 127).

In order to distinguish between virtual and real relative clauses it is necessary to look at *the Antecedent*.

The Antecedent

The Antecedent is the noun or pronoun in the main clause that the dependent relative clause is describing. Consider the following sentences:

(i) the man *whom you saw* is my father

    'the man . . . is my father' is the main clause;

    'whom you saw' is the relative clause.

    In this example, the relative clause is describing the subject of the main clause, i.e. 'the man'.

(ii) I danced with a girl who had danced with the Prince of Wales

    'I danced with a girl' is the main clause;

    'who had danced with the Prince of Wales' is the relative clause describing the object of the main clause, i.e. 'a girl'.

(iii) I know the place where they live

    'I know the place' is the main clause;

    'where they live' is a relative clause describing the object of the main clause, i.e. 'the place'.

In each of the first two examples, the relative clause is introduced by a relative pronoun; in the third example, it is introduced by a relative adverb.

The *antecedents* of the relative clauses in the examples quoted above are, respectively, 'the man'; 'a girl'; 'the place'.

There are two types of antecedent: defined and undefined. *Defined* antecedents are those which have the definite article (the), a numeral, or a demonstrative adjective (this, these) attached to them. *Undefined* antecedents have the indefinite article (a, an) or no article.

(A) *Relative clauses with undefined antecedents: Virtual relative clauses*

When the antecedent is *undefined*, almost any kind of sentence, both verbal and non-verbal, and including the forms discussed below (p. 120, ff.), may be juxtaposed directly to the main clause containing the antecedent, and be translated into English as a relative clause; there is no need for any introductory word:

e.g. (i) *sdm.f* in a relative clause:

she is a woman against whom lies are told

𓊃𓂋𓎛𓃰𓊪𓂧𓆑𓋴𓏤 𓏺

ḥmt pw ḏd grgw r.s

lit: main cl.: she is a woman (*ḥmt pw*)

rel. cl.: lies are told (*ḏd—sḏm.f*) against her

(ii) *sdm.n.f* in a relative clause:

I am speaking to a man who has eaten sycomore figs

𓂧𓂧𓏤𓈖𓋴𓏤𓄤𓇋𓈖𓆑𓎡𓃀𓅱 𓏼

ḏd.ỉ n s wnm.n.f k3w

lit: main cl.: I am speaking to a man (*ḏd. ỉ n s*)

rel. cl.: he has eaten (*wnm.n.f)* sycomore figs

(iii) non-verbal sentence in relative clause:

he is a god who has no equal

𓊹𓏤𓅱𓅧𓈖𓏤𓈖𓍱𓆑 𓏤𓏤

nṯr pw nn snnw.f

lit: main cl.: he is a god (*nṯr pw*)

rel. cl.: there is not (*nn*) his second (*snnw*)

(iv) the Stative in a relative clause:

she sat upon a throne which was wrought with gold

ḥms.n.s ḥr st b3k.tỉ m nbw

lit: main cl.: she sat upon a throne (*ḥms.n.s ḥr st*)

rel. cl.: it being wrought (*b3k.tỉ*) with gold

N.B. The antecedent in the main clause *must be picked up in the relative clause* by a pronoun (or, in the case of the Stative, by the appropriate ending): this pronoun is called *the Resumptive Pronoun* (see further below p. 122), which can be the subject of the verb in the relative clause (as in examples ii, iii and iv above) or be attached to a preposition (as in example i above) if the construction of the sentence demands it.

(B) *Relative clauses with defined antecedent: Real relative clauses*

When the antecedent is *defined*, the following relative clause *must* be a Real relative clause, which may be introduced in one of the following ways:

(1) by a relative adjective

(2) by a relative adjective allied to an adverb

(3) by a negative relative adjective

(4) by a *nisbe*-adjective

(5) by a participle

(6) by the relative form of a verb

(7) by the *sḏmty.fy* verb-form

N.B. Occasionally, relative clauses with *undefined* antecedents may be introduced in the ways listed above.

(B1) *The relative adjective*

As we saw on p. 117 in *English* relative clauses may be introduced by one of the relative pronouns (who, which, etc.). In *Egyptian*, there are no relative pronouns; instead, Egyptian employs a *relative adjective*, which has masculine and feminine forms:

m. sing. *nty*   f. sing. & plural *ntt*

m. plural *ntyw* (rare)

Uses of the relative adjective

(i) the relative adjective agrees with its antecedent in the main clause in number and gender:

e.g. 𓁐𓏥 ...

ḥmt tn ntt ḥmt.k

this woman who is your wife

'who is' is rendered by *ntt* (rel. adj. fem. sing.)

    to agree with 'woman'.

s nty m pr.ỉ

the man who is in my house

'who is' is rendered by *nty* (rel. adj. masc. sing.)

    to agree with 'man'.

(ii) the relative adjective can be used with a following verb-form (usually *sḏm.f* or *sḏm.n.f*) but its most common use is with non-verbal clauses with *adverbial predicate* (see p. 47); or with pseudo-verbal predicates, especially with the Stative (see p. 98) which seems to take the place of non-verbal clauses with adjectival predicates:

e.g.

ḥnrỉ nty m ḥnrt

the prisoner who is in the prison (adverb. predicate)

't nbt ntt mr.tỉ

every limb that is sore (Stative predicate)

N.B. Non-verbal clauses with *nominal* predicate are *never* introduced by the relative adjective.

(iii) the relative adjective can act as a noun, and as such be qualified by an adjective like ▽ *nb* 'all':

e.g.

pr.ỉ ḥn' ntt nb(t) ỉm.f

my house together with (*ḥn'*) whatever (*ntt nb(t)*) is in it *nty nb rn.f ỉm*

everyone whose name is here

(iv) if the subject of the relative clause *is identical* to the antecedent, the subject is not expressed since it is implicit in *nty, ntt,* etc.

Some students might find it useful to test whether the subject of the relative clause is identical with the antecedent in the following ways:

e.g. several women who were washing clothes

either:

(a) look at the subject of the main clause (women)

(b) decide which pronoun could replace the noun subject (they)

(c) insert the chosen pronoun after the relative pronoun (who)

(d) if the inserted pronoun then becomes the subject of the relative clause, then it and the antecedent are identical:

e.g. several women who (they) were washing clothes

or

(a) remove the relative pronoun

(b) insert the pronoun (they) that represents the subject of the main clause:

e.g. several women, they were washing clothes.

(v) if the subject of the relative clause *differs from* the antecedent, the antecedent must be expressed in the relative clause by a resumptive pronoun.

The Resumptive Pronoun

In each of the following examples, the relative clause does not have the same subject as the main clause:

e.g. (i) he is the man who I saw

(ii) he is the man whose son I saw

(iii) he is the man to whom I gave bread

In all the examples above, the subject of the main clause is 'the man' (as the complement of 'is'); but the subject of the relative clause is 'I'.

In *English*, the *case* of the relative pronoun changes when the subject of the relative clause differs from the antecedent:

e.g. (i) . . . the man *whom* I saw: relative pronoun 'whom' is object of 'I saw' and is therefore in the Accusative Case.

(ii) . . . the man *whose* son I saw: relative pronoun 'whose' indicates ownership and is therefore in the Genitive Case.

(iii) . . . the man *to whom I gave bread*: relative pronoun 'whom' is indirect object of verb (gave) and is therefore in the Dative Case.

In *Egyptian*, the relative adjective *does not have cases.* Instead, a pronoun, the so-called Resumptive Pronoun, is inserted into the relative clause; it picks up the antecedent and agrees with it in number and gender:

e.g. . . . the man whom I saw

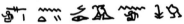

s nty m3.n.ỉ sw

lit: the man who I saw *him* (dep. pronoun *sw* as Resumptive)

. . . the man whose son I saw

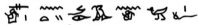

s nty m3.n.ỉ s3.f

lit: the man who I saw *his* son (suffix-pronoun *.f* as Resumptive)

. . . the man to whom I gave bread

s nty dỉ.n.ỉ n.f t

lit: the man who I gave bread *to him* (prep. plus suffix *.f* as Resumptive)

N.B. When the *subject* of the relative clause is a *pronoun*, the dependent pronouns are used:

e.g. this condition in which I was

ssm pn nty wỉ ẖr.f

lit: this condition which I was under it

(B2) *The relative adjective allied to an adverb*

The English relative adverb (see p. 117) can be rendered in Egyptian by a relative adjective plus an adverb; the adverb is known as a *Resumptive* Adverb in that it picks up a noun in the main clause:

e.g. the place where His Majesty was

bw nty ḥm.f ỉm

lit: the place which His Majesty was there (*ỉm*—adverb)

(B3) *The negative relative adjective*

A common word for 'who/which . . . not' is the negative relative adjective which has the following forms:

ỉwty

ỉwtt

Uses of the negative relative adjective

(i) *ỉwty/ỉwtt* is used in the same way as *nty* etc. It is most frequently found with a following *sḏm.f* form:

e.g. *s pw ỉwty sḏm.f n ḥmt.f*

he is the man who does not listen to his wife

ḥmt pw ỉwtt ḏd.s n ḥỉ.s

she is the woman who does not speak to her husband

(ii) the negative relative adjective is used to make up the following common phrases:

(a) *ntt ỉwtt* 'that which exists and that which does not exist' i.e. everything

(b) *ỉwty sw* 'who is not a him' i.e. a nonentity

(c) *ỉwty n.f* 'who has not belonging to him' i.e. who has nothing.

(B4) *Nisbe-adjective*

As we saw on p. 14 relative adjectives can be formed from nouns and prepositions: *ḥry* 'who is on' or 'over' (from prep.);

ḥnty 'who is before' or 'who is at the head of' (from prep. 𓍿𓄑𓏏𓐍 ～) ﹐ 𓐍𓏏𓄑
ỉmy 'who is in' or 'among' (from prep. 𓄑) etc.:

e.g. 𓎝 𓈖 𓄿𓐍𓏏𓄑 𓂋𓏤

   w'b ỉmy pr.f

   the priest who is in his house

(B5) *Participles*

In *English*, a participle is an *adjective* derived from a verb (and sometimes called a Gerundive):

e.g. the team, *hearing* the result, cheered

   ('hearing', participle derived from verb 'hear', describes 'team')

the government, *having been defeated*, resigned

   ('having been defeated', participle derived from verb 'defeat', describes 'government')

In *Egyptian*, a participle is not only a *verbal adjective* but also a *verbal noun* (sometimes called a Gerund):

e.g. 𓄔𓄑𓅓𓅱   *sḏmw* 'the listener' (from verb 𓄔𓄑 *sḏm* 'hear').

Compare the English 'eating people is wrong' where 'eating' is a participle derived from the verb 'eat' and acting as a noun (see p. 85).

Types of Participle in Egyptian

In Egyptian, participles have an active or a passive voice; and imperfective and perfective tenses, with the imperfective tense suggesting the idea of continuing action, repetition, custom, but the perfective tense marking a completed action that has normally taken place in the past.

Forms of the Participles

Originally, participles may have had a variety of different endings. However, these endings were seldom written out in hieroglyphic script and we are often left to determine voice and tense from context only. Tense at least is often indicated in the *weak verbs* (see p. 56): here, the general rule is that *gemination indicates imperfective tense*; perfective participles *do not* geminate.

Broadly speaking, the participial endings are as follows:

participle:	active		passive	
imperfective	𓇌 or 𓏭 -y (m. sing.)		𓅱 -w (m. sing. & plural)	
	𓇌𓅱 -yw	(m. plur.)		
	𓏏 -t	(fem. sing. & plural)	𓏏 -t	(f. sing. & plural)
perfective	none	(m. sing.)	𓇌 -y	(m. sing.)
	𓅱 -w	(m. plural)	none	(m. plural)
	𓏏 -t	(fem. sing. & plural)	none	(fem. sing. & plural)

N.B. Participles agree in number and gender with the noun/pronoun to which
    they are attached.

Uses of the Participles

The participles may be used as i) nouns or ii) adjectives.

(i) participles as nouns: when used as a noun, a participle is often given an
    appropriate determinative:

    e.g.   [hieroglyphs] *hsy* a blessed man (m. sing. participle)

        [hieroglyphs] *msddt* a hated woman (f. sing. participle)

(ii) participles as adjectives: when used as an adjective, the Egyptian participle
    is equivalent to a relative clause. The examples above could equally well
    have been translated as 'a man who is blessed' and 'a woman who is hated'.
    Participles are used as relative clauses *only when the subject of the relative*
    clause is identical with the antecedent:

    e.g. [hieroglyphs]

        ntr mrr rmt

        a god who loves men

        (imperfective active participle—*mrr*—masc. sing.)

        [hieroglyphs]

        nfrt nbt ỉnnt n nb.ỉ

        every good thing which was brought to my lord

        (imperfective passive participle—*ỉnnt*—fem. sing.)

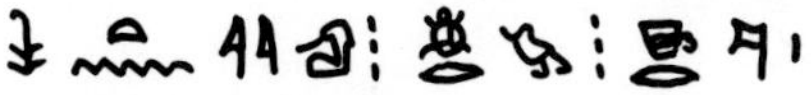

nsyw ḫprw ḏr nṯr

the kings who had existed since the time of the god

(perfective active participle—*ḫprw*—masc. plural)

ỉnb ỉry r ḥsf ḫftyw

the wall which had been made to repulse enemies

(perfective passive participle—*ỉry*—masc. sing.)

N.B. Sometimes, a participle is used with the *m* of predication as an epithet:

e.g. a heart capable of suffering

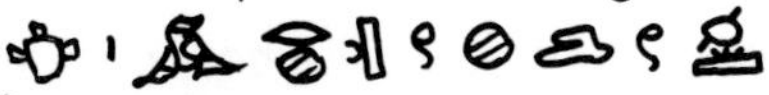

ỉb m rḫ wḫdw

lit: a heart which is as one who knows suffering

(B6) *The Relative Form*

When the subject of a relative clause was *different from the antecedent,* the Egyptians were able to employ a special form of the verb known as 'the Relative Form'. This Form seems to have been peculiar to Egyptian—English, for instance, does not have a relative form of the verb.

Verbs being used in their Relative Form have a variety of special endings to indicate imperfective and perfective tenses, and a masculine and feminine writing, as follows:

(i) *Imperfective Relative Form*

	strong verbs		*weak verbs* (geminate)	
masc.	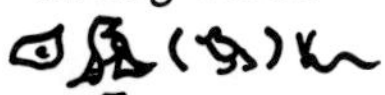	*sḏm(w).f*	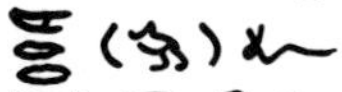	*mrr(w).f*
fem.		*sḏmt.f*		*mrrt.f*

N.B. The  of the masculine is often not written out, especially before suffix-pronoun subjects.

(ii) *Perfective Relative Form*

Earlier writings

masc.  *sḏmy.f*

fem.  *sḏmty.f*

Later writings

masc. 〔hieroglyphs〕 *sḏm(w).n.f*

fem. 〔hieroglyphs〕 *sḏmt.n.f*

Uses of the Relative Form

(i) Imperfective Relative Form: usually stresses repeated or continuous action in the *present tense* (sometimes past, rarely future):

e.g. 〔hieroglyphs〕

s rḏỉ(w).ỉ n.f t

the man to whom I give bread (lit: the man which I give to him bread)

(ii) Perfective Relative Form:

(a) the earlier form was used to describe both past and future events:

e.g. 〔hieroglyphs〕

ỉw nb h3y.ỉ r.f

every island to which I went

(lit: every island which I went to it)

〔hieroglyphs〕

sḏm n ḏdty.ỉ n.k

listen to what I shall say to you

(b) the later form (often called the *sḏmw.n.f* relative form) was used to describe completed past action:

e.g. 〔hieroglyphs〕

ỉnw pn ỉn(w).n.ỉ m ỉw pn

this tribute which I brought from the island

(iii) Like the participles, the Relative forms may be used as nouns:

e.g. 〔hieroglyphs〕

ḏdt m pr.f

what was said in his house

(B7) *The sḏm ty.fy*

If you have a relative clause where

(i) the subject is identical with the antecedent

(ii) the verb is active

(iii) the verb is in the *future* tense

then a special form of the verb called the *sḏmty.fy* may be used.

The *sḏmty-fy* is formed from the stem of the verb, to which is added ⟨glyph⟩ *ty* and the following pronouns (derived from the suffix-pronouns):

masc. sing. ⟨glyph⟩ *fy*

fem. sing. ⟨glyph⟩ *sy*

plural (common) ⟨glyph⟩ *sn.*

Sometimes the *ty* is abbreviated, as is the pronoun:

e.g. ⟨glyph⟩ ; ⟨glyph⟩ ; ⟨glyph⟩ (m. sing.)

⟨glyph⟩ ; ⟨glyph⟩ (f. sing.)

⟨glyph⟩ ; ⟨glyph⟩ ; ⟨glyph⟩ (plural)

N.B. These endings are normally written *after* the determinative of the verb, but the abbreviation ⟨glyph⟩ often precedes it.

Uses of the sḏmty.fy

(i) the *sḏmty.fy* can be used as an adjective that expresses the quality or attributes of the noun it describes (i.e. as an epithet) but it is most often used as a substitute for the non-existent future active participle:

e.g. ⟨hieroglyphs⟩

srw ỉwty.sn r bỉ3 pn

officials who shall come to this mining region

⟨hieroglyphs⟩

h3st wnnty.sy ḥr mw.f

a country which will be loyal to him (*ḥr mw.f* lit: on his water)

(ii) the *sḏmty.fy* can be used as a noun; and when so used may be qualified by ⟨glyph⟩ *nb* 'every', 'all', etc.:

e.g. ⟨hieroglyphs⟩

sw3t(y).fy nb ḥr wḏ pn

everyone who shall pass by this stele

EXERCISE 17

(a) *Write in hieroglyphs and transliteration*

    1. How happy is a king who is at the head of his army.

    2. He saw a gate before which two obelisks wrought with electrum were erected.

    3. The place in which my heart spends the day.

    4. O scribes who shall enter this tomb, who shall see what is in it.

    5. I seized all that was in his town.

(b) *Translate into English*

    1. [hieroglyphs]

    2. [hieroglyphs]

    3. [hieroglyphs]

    (*m-ỉsw*—in exchange for) [hieroglyphs]

    4. [hieroglyphs]

    5. [hieroglyphs]

Chapter 18

WORD ORDER AND EMPHASIS

Word Order

The normal word order in Egyptian verbal sentences, when both subject and object are *nouns*, is 1) verb 2) subject 3) object 4) dative 5) adverb or adverbial phrase.

However, if the subject, object or dative is or contains a *pronoun*, then the following rules apply:

(i) the verb must come first

(ii) a noun must not precede a pronoun

(iii) a dependent pronoun must not precede a suffix-pronoun

(iv) when a sentence contains a dative made up of ‿‿‿ plus a suffix-pronoun, the dative is placed immediately after the verb, taking precedence over a *noun* subject; and over the object even if the object is a pronoun

(v) if the subject is a *pronoun* (suffix) a pronominal dative (‿‿‿ plus suffix) is placed immediately after the subject, and precedes the object even if this be a (dependent) pronoun.

The adverbial phrase can be put out of its normal position at the end of the sentence; note the following instances:

(1) if the *object* is particularly long, the adverbial phrase may precede it:

e.g.

ỉr.n.f m mnw.f n ỉt.f sʿḥ' ṯḥnwy wrwy bnbnt m ḏʿm

he made as his monument for his father the erecting (*sʿḥ'*) of two great obelisks which had pyramidions of electrum—the adverbial phrase *m mnw.f* (as his monument) takes precedence over the multi-worded object, *sʿḥ'* etc.

(2) if the adverbial phrase forms an expression inseparable from the verb, it may precede
   a noun subject: e.g. ⟨glyphs⟩ *rdỉ m ỉb* 'put in the heart' i.e. 'inspire':

e.g. ⟨glyphs⟩

   rdỉ m ỉb.ỉ nṯr ỉr.ỉ mnw.f

   god inspired me to make his monument.

The following table illustrates the permutations of word order in a verbal sentence:

	Verb	Subject: noun	Object: noun	Dative: ⁓ + noun	Adverb or adverbial phrase
A	⟨glyph⟩ *dỉ*	⟨glyph⟩ *nb*	⟨glyph⟩ *t*	⟨glyph⟩ *n ḥkr*	⟨glyph⟩ *m nỉwt.f*
	Verb	Subject: suffix pronoun	Object: noun	Dative: ⁓ + noun	Adverb or adverbial phrase
B	⟨glyph⟩ *dỉ*	⟨glyph⟩ *f*	⟨glyph⟩ *t*	⟨glyph⟩ *n ḥkr*	⟨glyph⟩ *m nỉwt.f*
	Verb	Subject: suffix pronoun	Object: dep. pronoun	Dative: ⁓ + noun	Adverb or adverbial phrase
C	⟨glyph⟩ *dỉ*	⟨glyph⟩ *f*	⟨glyph⟩ *sw*	⟨glyph⟩ *n ḥkr*	⟨glyph⟩ *m nỉwt.f*
	Verb	Subject: suffix pronoun	Dative: ⁓ + suffix	Object: dep. pronoun	Adverb or adverbial phrase
D	⟨glyph⟩ *dỉ*	⟨glyph⟩ *f*	⟨glyph⟩ *n.f*	⟨glyph⟩ *sw*	⟨glyph⟩ *m nỉwt.f*
	Verb	Subject: suffix pronoun	Dative: ⁓ + suffix	Object: noun	Adverb or adverbial phrase
E	⟨glyph⟩ *dỉ*	⟨glyph⟩ *f*	⟨glyph⟩ *n.f.*	⟨glyph⟩ *t*	⟨glyph⟩ *m nỉwt.f*
	Verb	Dative: ⁓ + suffix	Subject: noun	Object: noun	Adverb or adverbial phrase
F	⟨glyph⟩ *dỉ*	⟨glyph⟩ *n.f.*	⟨glyph⟩ *nb*	⟨glyph⟩ *t*	⟨glyph⟩ *m nỉwt.f*

	Verb	Dative: 〰〰〰 + suffix	Object: dep. pronoun	Subject: noun	Adverb or adverbial phrase
G	◁◻ *dỉ*	〰〰〰 *n.f.*	*sw*	*nb*	*m nỉwt.f*

	Verb	Object: dep. pronoun	Subject: noun	Dative: 〰〰〰 + noun	Adverb or adverbial phrase
H	◁◻ *dỉ*	*sw*	*nb*	〰〰〰 *n ḥkr*	*m nỉwt.f*

A. The master gives bread to the hungry in his city.

B. He gives bread to the hungry in his city.

C. He gives it to the hungry in his city.

D. He gives it to him in his city.

E. He gives him bread in his city.

F. The master gives him bread in his city.

G. The master gives it to him in his city.

H. The master gives it to the hungry in his city.

e.g.

nb dỉ.f t n ḥkr

(as for) the master, he gives bread to the hungry

(subject *nb* (master) in anticipatory emphasis (see p. 135); resumptive pronoun—suffix *f*—is subject of verb)

alternative English version: the *master* gives bread to the hungry

t dỉ sw nb n ḥkr

(as for) bread, the master gives it to the hungry

(object *t* (bread) in anticipatory emphasis; resumptive pronoun—dependent pronoun *sw*—is object of verb).

alternative English version: the master gives *bread* to the hungry

Emphasis

If an English-speaking person wishes to draw a *reader's* attention to any particular part
of a sentence, he can:

(1) underline a phrase or word in it

(2) use italics

(3) use punctuation: a dash or a comma, e.g. 'he gives bread to the hungry—in the city'
   where the use of the dash before 'in the city' emphasises that he gave bread in the
   city rather than elsewhere.

A *listener's* attention may be drawn to a particular part of a sentence by the tone of voice
used by a reader.

   Although the Egyptians did not use punctuation, they also had ways of indicating
emphasis; they could:

(1) invert the normal order of words

(2) use a particle or preposition to draw attention to a word or group of words

(3) use a special verb-form to draw attention to the last part of the sentence, that is, to
   the adverb or adverbial phrase.

(1) *Inversion of the normal word order*

   The most emphatic positions in a sentence are either at the beginning or at the end
   of it. If a reader finds something at the beginning of a sentence that he did not expect
   to find there, then he notices it, partly because he reads it first, partly because it is
   unexpected. The end of a sentence is also a good place for throwing phrases into
   relief.

   In *Egyptian* sentences, it is the verb that one normally expects to find at the beginning
   of a sentence. However, a noun, or an adverb or adverbial phrase, can be removed
   from its normal position in a sentence and put at the beginning of it. This device is
   known as *Anticipatory Emphasis*.

   It should be noted that when a noun is taken out of its normal place in a sentence,
   then the verb is left without its noun subject or noun object. It must accordingly be
   supplied with one in the form of a *Resumptive pronoun*.

Anticipatory emphasis in verbal sentences

(1) (a) a *noun subject* can be placed at the beginning of the sentence:

e.g. 𓈗𓂋𓄿𓏤𓏛𓏛𓈖𓂝𓏤𓅱 ...

mw swr̃.tw.f mr.k

(as for) the water, it is drunk when you wish

or

the *water* is drunk when you wish

(b) a *pronoun subject* can be placed at the beginning of the sentence; in this case, the independent pronouns are used with *sḏm.f* or *sḏm.n.f*:

e.g. 𓄿𓇋𓈖𓄿𓉐𓂋𓈖𓏤𓅓𓉐

ʾink pr.n.ʾi m pr

It is I who have come forth from the house

(2) a noun *object* can be placed at the beginning of the sentence:

e.g. �

snty.k dʾi.n.ʾi sn h3.k

(as for) your sisters, I have placed them around you

or

I have placed *your sisters* around you

(3) an *adverbial phrase* can be placed at the beginning of the sentence:

e.g. �glyphs

m-ḫt nn wḏ3 ḥm.f r pr-nsw

after this, His Majesty proceeded to the palace

Anticipatory emphasis in non-verbal sentences

(1) the *subject* can be placed at the beginning of the sentence:

e.g. �glyphs

ʾntyw n.ʾi-ʾim sw

(as for) the incense, it belongs to me

(2) *Use of preposition or particle for emphasis*

(i) the preposition 𓇋𓂋 *ʾir* 'as for', 'as to': when *ʾir* is placed before a group of words standing in anticipatory emphasis at the head of a sentence, it is often being used to lighten the sentence by placing outside it some lengthy or cumbrous phrase; on the other hand, the same device can be used to draw attention to the phrase:

e.g. 𓂋𓏤𓊖𓄿 ... 𓂋 𓊪 ... 𓈖 𓎡

ỉr ḥm nb r pn n ꜥḳ.n.f

as for anyone who does not know this spell, he shall not enter

(ii) the enclitic particle ꜥꜣ *rf*, often used in conjunction with 𓇋𓏏𓀢 ỉst 'lo', may be employed to emphasise a whole sentence, the inference being that there will be a further development:

e.g. 𓂧𓂋𓀢𓈖𓊪𓏏𓈖𓈖 ...

ỉst rf ỉn.n.sn mnỉwt.sn

now when they had brought their necklaces . . .

(they presented them to the king)

(iii) the non-enclitic particle 𓇋𓈖 ỉn 'indeed' may be used in conjunction with a participle, in a special construction known as *the Participial Statement,* in order to throw emphasis upon a noun subject. The construction of the Participial Statement is:

ỉn *plus* a noun *plus* a participle,

> which *must* be active,
>
> *can be* perfective or imperfective,
>
> and is invariable in number & gender

(a) participial statement with perfective active participle for *past* tense:

e.g. 𓇋𓈖 𓍲𓏤 𓂋𓂝 𓁹

ỉn ḥm.f rdỉ ỉr.t(w).f

it was His Majesty who caused it to be made

(lit: indeed His Majesty was the one who caused . . .)

(b) participial statement with imperfective active participle for *present* tense:

e.g. 𓇋𓈖 𓊹𓏤 𓂋𓂋𓄿𓂋

ỉn nṯr ỉrr ỉkr

it is god who makes prosperity

N.B. 𓇋𓈖 plus *sḏm.f* is used for *future* tense (see p. 5)

(iv) The Participial Statement may be used to throw emphasis upon a pronoun subject. The construction is the same as that outlined in section iii) except that ⌇ is not used. The pronoun subject is expressed by an independent pronoun:

e.g.

ỉnk š'd drt.f

it was I who cut off its (elephant) trunk

(š'd—perfective active participle)

ntsn dd n.ỉ mw

it is they who give me water

(dd—imperfective active participle)

(3) *Emphasis using special verb-form*

In Chapter 8, the reader was introduced to Egyptian verb groups; and to the fact that weak verbs in the *sḏm.f* form sometimes geminate (see p. 59). Older grammars defined this gemination as referring to incomplete, recurrent action and thought of it as marking an imperfective tense, as it does in geminating participles. It has been argued that this is not the case and that gemination in the *sḏm.f* can indicate emphasis.

In Coptic, the latest development of the Ancient Egyptian language which used the Greek alphabet rather than hieroglyphs and, unlike Egyptian, wrote down vowel sounds (see IEH p. 48) it is quite clear that certain tenses of the verb have *two* versions (called First and Second Tenses). For example, using as a model the verb 'to hear', which is   *sḏm* in Middle Egyptian and CWTM (pronounced so-tem) in Coptic, the tenses are:

	Tense 1		Tense 2	
Present	ϤϹⲰⲦⲘ	*and*	ⲈϤϹⲰⲦⲘ	
	(f-so-tem)		(ef-so-tem)	— he hears
Perfect	ⲀϤϹⲰⲦⲘ	*and*	ⲚⲦⲀϤϹⲰⲦⲘ	
	(af-so-tem)		(ent-af-so-tem)	— he heard

Future   ⲩⲛⲁ̀ⲥⲱⲧⲙ   *and*   ⲉⲩⲛⲁ̀ⲥⲱⲧⲙ

          (f-na-so-tem)   (ef-na-so-tem)   — he will hear

Habitude   ⲩⲁⲩⲥⲱⲧⲙ   *and*   ⲉⲩⲁⲩⲥⲱⲧⲙ

          (shaf-so-tem)   (esh-af-so-tem)   — he is wont to hear

The special function of the second tenses was discovered in 1944 by Polotsky who compared the Coptic versions of the Gospels with the Greek originals and found that where the Copts used a second tense, the Greeks used an emphatic form of the verb. He deduced that the purpose of the Second Tense in Coptic was to throw stress upon, to emphasise, an adverbial phrase which, in Coptic as in Middle Egyptian, is written at the end of the sentence. It was known that Late Egyptian had a Second or Emphatic, Tense: *ỉ:ỉr.f sḏm*. The question then became: did Middle Egyptian have a Second Tense, and, if so, how could it be recognised.

There is in fact *no outward sign of a Second Tense with strong verbs* or with *sḏm.n.f* in Middle Egyptian. The task is made easier with weak verbs, which geminate, it is thought, in order to indicate a Second Tense. However, even here the matter is not straightforward: gemination in verbs in the *sḏm.f* can denote that the verb should be translated as a circumstantial tense (see p. 59).

Obviously, a prerequisite for a geminating verb in the *sḏm.f*-form to indicate a Second Tense is that the sentence should have an adverb or an adverbial phrase: without such a phrase, there would be no point in having a Second Tense, the purpose of which is to throw emphasis on an adverbial phrase (called the *Adverbial Extension*). In cases such as this, the verb should be translated as part of a clause of circumstance: e.g.

ḥꜥ.sn m33.sn tw

they rejoice when they see you

Second Tenses in Middle Egyptian

A weak verb may geminate in the *sḏm.f* form in order to throw emphasis on an adverbial extension, which may be an adverb, an adverbial phrase (preposition plus noun) or an interrogative word. The construction was useful in both written and spoken Egyptian since the way in which the verb at the beginning of a sentence was written or pronounced immediately drew attention to the fact that the crux of the sentence was going to come in the adverbial extension at the end. By using a verb in the Second Tense, the Egyptians were able to throw emphasis upon the adverbial extension *without upsetting the normal word order* of the sentence, which places the verb at the beginning and the adverbial extension at the end. English, of course, does not have a second tense, and so, when translating the Egyptian Second Tense it becomes necessary in English to transfer the adverbial extension to the beginning of the sentence in order to emphasize it. For instance, a normal tense could be translated into English as 'I went into the town'; but a Second Tense would have to be translated as 'It was into the town that I went.'

e.g.   *prĭ* 'to go'

pr s r nĭwt

verb shows no gemination, translation therefore is

the man goes to town

prr s r nĭwt

verb does show gemination, translation therefore is

it is to town that the man goes

Geminating sḏm.f in statements

Geminating *sḏm.f* is found emphasising an adverbial extension in past, present and future tenses, active voice; in Middle Egyptian, however, a Second Tense is found relatively infrequently in past tense:

e.g. Present tense:

dd.tw n.k ĭrty.ky r m33

it is in order to see (*r m33*—adverbial extension formed from preposition and infinitive, which is a noun) that your eyes are given (*dd.tw*—geminating *sḏm.f* of verb *dĭ*) to you

Past tense:

ỉb.f ỉrr.t(w) r ḥsf n.f

he thought (*ỉb.f*) that it was in order to punish him (*r ḥsf n.f*—adverbial extension composed of *r* plus infinitive (*ḥsf*)) that it was done (*ỉrr.t(w)*—geminating *sḏm.f*)

Future tense:

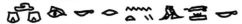

dgg.k r nty m-bȝḥ.k

it is at what is before you that you should look

Geminating sḏm.f in questions

The interrogative word is placed at the end of the sentence, and is in fact an adverbial extension:

e.g. 𓎛𓎼𓏏𓆑𓏲𓏭𓂋𓂋𓏏𓊪𓇓𓄣𓁷𓅓

ḥnwt.ỉ ỉrr.t pȝ ỉb ḥr-m

my lady, why are you in this mood?

(lit: my lady (vocative) you are making (*ỉrr*) this mood (*ỉb*) on account of what (*ḥr-m*))

EXERCISE 18

(a) *Write in hieroglyphs and transliteration*

   1. His beard, it was longer than two cubits.
   2. It was my lord who sent the gold but you were the one who gave it to me.
   3. It is the woman who gives it to him.
   4. Why is the priest going into the temple?
   5. It is to my son that these things should be given.

(b) *Translate into English*

   1. [hieroglyphs]
   2. [hieroglyphs]
   3. [hieroglyphs]
   4. [hieroglyphs]

Chapter 19

NEGATION

Egyptian was rich in negative words and the reader has already encountered the two most common of them, 〰️ *nn* and 〰️ *n*, in the following instances:

〰️ is used: to negate *sdm.f* (when it has future meaning; see IEH p. 105)

to convey the meaning '*not* to own', '*not* to have'; (see p. 39)

to negate non-verbal sentences with nominal predicate; (see p. 45)

to negate non-verbal sentences with adjectival predicate; (see p. 47)

to negate non-verbal sentences with adverbial predicate and nominal subject (see p. 48)

with 〰️ (*nn wn*) to express universal denial 'there is not' (see p. 50)

with *sdm.f* to supply negation for Pseudo-verbal construction (see p. 104)

〰️ is used: to negate *sdm.f* (when it has past meaning; see IEH p. 105)

to negate *sdm.n.f* (when it has present meaning; see IEH p. 105)

to negate non-verbal sentences with adjectival predicate (see p. 47)

to negate non-verbal sentences with adverbial predicate and pronoun subject (see p. 49)

with *sdm.n.f* to supply negation for Pseudo-verbal Construction (see p. 104)

The use of *nn* and *n* is almost confined to statements and certain subordinate clauses, as is the use of the negative relative adjective 𓂜𓈖𓏲𓏏𓇌/𓂜𓂋𓏲𓏏𓏏 *iwty/iwtt*(see p. 124). In other cases, Egyptian uses a *negative verb*.

The negative verb

Egyptian has two special negative verbs, ✝🐦👄 *ꞌmꞌ* and 👄🐦 *tm*, which are used in the following way: the negative verb *precedes* the verb that is being negated, which then becomes what is known as the 'negatival complement'. It is the negative verb that is then conjugated (i.e. takes a noun or *suffix*-pronoun as its subject) although the negatival complement remains a verb in that it can take an *object* of its own (which can be a noun or a *dependent* pronoun). The negatival complement sometimes has the ending 🐦 *w*, although this is not often written.

A. *The negative verb* ✝🐦👄 *ꞌmꞌ*

ꞌmꞌ has the meaning 'not to be' and has two uses:

(1) it can be used in its *sḏm.f*-form to express a negative wish or command:

e.g. ✝🐦👄 👄🐦👄🐦

ꞌm.k wsr m ẖt.s

you may not be powerful in her womb

(*ꞌm.k*: negative verb ✝🐦👄 in *sḏm.f*-form, with suffix-pronoun *.k* as subject; *wsr*: negatival complement)

N.B. There seems to have been a reluctance to separate the negatival complement from the negative verb with anything more substantial than a suffix-pronoun, consequently, when the subject of the negative verb is a *noun* it is placed *after* the negatival complement:

e.g. ✝🐦👄👄🐦👄🐦

ꞌmꞌ m33 rmṯ

let not men see

(*ꞌmꞌ*—negative verb; *m33*—negatival complement; *rmṯ*—subject of negative verb)

(2) the *imperative* form of *ꞌmꞌ*, which is 🐦 *m*, is used to negate an imperative:

e.g. 🐦👄🐦

m snḏ

do not be afraid

B. *The negative verb*  *tm*

tm has a much wider variety of uses than the negative verb *ỉmỉ*. In its *sḏm.f*-form, it can be used in both main and subordinate clauses; but its most important function is to negate the so-called nominal parts of the verb (i.e. the grammatical constructions that are nouns formed from verbs): the infinitive (see p. 85); the participles (see p. 125); the relative form (see p. 127); the *sḏm.ty.fy* (see p. 128).

1. *tm in main clauses*

 (a) in questions employing an interrogative word (but *not* after 𓇋𓈖 *ỉn*):

  e.g. 𓂝𓏏𓈖 𓉔𓂋𓅓

  tm.t ẖn ḥr-m

  why do you not row?

 (b) in double negatives (where *tm* is often best translated as 'fail'):

  e.g.

  n tm.f wšb

  he does not fail to answer

 (c) after particles such as 𓇋𓐍 *ỉẖ* 'then', 'therefore' (see p. 6):

  e.g.

  ỉẖ tm sḏm nb.ỉ

  then my lord will not hear

2. *tm in subordinate clauses*

 (a) in conditional clauses after 𓇋𓂋 *ỉr*:

  e.g.

  ỉr tm.f snḏ

  if he is not afraid

 (b) after prepositions:

  e.g.

  r tm.s mdw

  so that she does not speak

 (c) in virtual clauses of result or purpose:

  e.g.

  tm spr bw-ḏw r.k

  lest evil reach you

3. *tm as negation of nominal parts of the verb*

(a) *tm* negates the infinitive:

e.g. 𓊡𓂝𓏏𓃾𓏺

tm wnm ḥs

not to eat excrement

(b) *tm* negates participles:

e.g. 𓊡𓂝𓏺𓍿𓏺

tm ỉr n.f krs

who had not made a coffin for himself

(c) *tm* negates the relative form:

e.g. 𓊡𓂝𓏺𓍿𓏺

tmt.n.ỉ ỉr mnw ỉm.s

in which I have not made monuments

(d) *tm* negates the *sḏm.ty.fy* (by being put into the *sḏm.ty.fy* itself):

e.g. 𓊡𓂝𓏺𓍿𓏺

tm.ty.fy ꜥḥꜣ ḥr.f

he who shall not fight on behalf of it

C. *The negative construction* 𓈖𓊃𓊪 *n sp*

Many of the examples given above could have been translated more emphatically as 'never' instead of 'not'. 'Never' can be indicated more precisely by the use of

𓈖𓊃𓊪 *n sp sḏm.f*:

e.g. 𓈖𓊃𓊪 𓏺𓍿𓏺

n sp ỉwt ḫt ỉm.ỉ

never was there any shortcoming in me

(lit: never did anything come in me)

EXERCISE 19

(a) *Write in hieroglyphs and transliteration*

1. It is not a burden upon your arms.

2. Never had the like been done since primaeval times.

3. Why do you not listen to me?

4. Do not defraud the poor man of his possessions.

5. There is none whose possessions I took away.

(b) *Translate into English*

Chapter 20

Part 1

THE EGYPTIAN CALENDAR

The Egyptian year, called 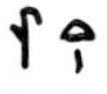 *rnpt*, was divided into twelve months ( *3bd*), each with thirty days ( *hrw*). The Egyptians recognised that this left their civil year out of step with the astronomical year, and attempted to solve the problem by adding five epagomenal or extra days to it. They did not realise, or so it seems, that this left their year $\frac{1}{4}$ of a day short, with the result that four years after the day when the civil year began at the same time as the astronomical year, the years were one day out of step, with the civil year beginning one day earlier than the astronomical year.

We solve this problem by not having regular thirty-day months; and by adding an extra day to our month of February every fourth, or Leap, year. The Egyptians never used this device, and the astronomical year gradually fell further and further behind their civil year: it would be 1460 years before they coincided again. One interesting result of this is that from time to time the real summer fell in the winter of the civil year, and *vice versa*, a fact which is obvious in some ancient records, such as that of the mining expedition to Sinai to prospect for turquoise undertaken by Harwerre, during the reign of Amenemhat III (1842–1797 B.C.). Harwerre states that his expedition took place in 'the third month of Peret' (see below), normally considered to be a winter month. However, according to Harwerre, 'It was difficult, in my opinion, to find the right colour when the desert was hot in summer'—obviously, Harwerre's expedition took place in the real summer although the civil calendar stated that it was winter!

The twelve months of the Egyptian year were numbered and allotted to seasons, called 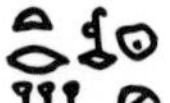 *tr*, each of four months duration:

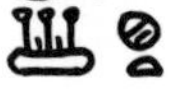 *3ḫt* Inundation season (the time when the Nile flood covered Egypt)

𓄿𓂝 *prt* Winter season   (the time when the land gradually emerged from the flood water)

𓇓𓈗𓇳 *šmw* Summer season   (writing perhaps derived from noun 𓇓𓄿𓅱 *šw* 'lack', plus 𓈗 *mw*, 'water', giving *šw mw* 'lack of water')

The Inundation officially began on 19th July (Julian calendar) every year, and marked the Egyptian New Year's Day (𓍹 *wp-rnpt*: the Opening of the Year). At the same time, the dog-star, Sirius, which had been invisible for a time, appeared again in the sky, shining brilliantly on the horizon. Modern astronomers call this the Heliacal rising of Sirius; the Egyptians, who identified Sirius with the goddess, Sothis, called it 'the going up of Sothis' (𓇓𓂦𓇼 *prt spdt*).

From the Persian period (from 525 B.C.) the months were given Greek names instead of numbers, the names being derived from feasts. For example, the feast of the goddess, Ernutet (in Greek, Thermouthis), gave its name to the month called Pharmouthi, although the feast actually took place in the following month (Pakhons).

If the Heliacal rising of Sirius had always formed the beginning of the Egyptian year, the following would be the corresponding months in Julian calendar terms:

Julian calendar	Greek name	Egyptian season	
July	Thouth	Month 1	*3ḥt*
August	Phaophi	Month 2	*3ḥt*
September	Athyr	Month 3	*3ḥt*
October	Khoiak	Month 4	*3ḥt*
November	Tybi	Month 1	*prt*
December	Mekhir	Month 2	*prt*
January	Phamenoth	Month 3	*prt*
February	Pharmouthi	Month 4	*prt*
March	Pakhons	Month 1	*šmw*
April	Payni	Month 2	*šmw*
May	Epiph	Month 3	*šmw*
June	Mesore	Month 4	*šmw*

The correct way to refer to the months of the Egyptian year is as follows:

e.g. *3bd 4 prt*   fourth month of Winter (or peret)

3bd 2 3ḫt   second month of Inundation (or akhet)

3bd 3 šmw third month of Summer (or shomu)

N.B. The first day of the month was often referred to as *tpy*, often written with the genitival *n*:

e.g. *tpy (n) 3ḫt* first month of Inundation

Days and dates

Days

The Egyptians were the first to divide the day into twenty-four hours which they called (var.   ) *wnwt*. Although they allotted twelve hours to the day and twelve to the night, the length of the hour was not very precise: the Egyptians had no words for minutes and seconds and referred to 'an instant of time' or 'a moment' only, using the term   *3t*. The hours were often measured by means of sun-dials or clepsydra (water clocks), but their length varied according to season, being longer in summer than in winter.

Dates

In dates, the word   *rnpt* is not used for 'year'; instead, the Egyptians used the expression   . The first two hieroglyphs in this group are the same as those used to write *rnpt* (, see above). However, they are *transliterated* as ḥ3t sp and originally referred to the biennial cattle census which was carried out in Egypt, and which was used as the great event by which the years were measured:

e.g.

ḥ3t sp 4 ṯnwt ỉḥ

beginning of the fourth time of the counting (*ṯnwt*) of the oxen.

At some time during the Old Kingdom, the Egyptians began to base their dates on the years of a king's reign; they never used a continuous era. Thus, what we would describe as 1358 B.C., in Egyptian would appear as Regnal Year 2 of Tutankhamun.

In dates, the word for 'day' is *never* 𓏏𓇿𓏤 *hrw* but 𓏏𓇿𓇳 *sw*, usually abbreviated to 𓇳 :

e.g. 𓊪 𓎡 𓏥 𓇿𓇿𓇿 𓇳𓇳 𓇳 𓈖𓈖𓈖 𓏤 𓋹 (𓏤𓏤 𓋹)

     h3t sp 2 3bd 3 3ht sw 1 hr hm n nsw-bit (n-m3't-r')

     regnal year 2, month 3 of Inundation, day 1 under (*hr*) the Majesty of the King of Upper and Lower Egypt (N-maat-Re), i.e. Amenemhat III

The Titulary of the King

The royal titulary (𓈖𓎡𓃀𓏏 *nhbt*) consisted of five 'great names' (𓂋𓈖 𓅨 *rn wr* (singular)) which were assumed by a king on the day of his accession to the throne. The reader was introduced to the last two of these names in Lesson 6 of IEH. The other three names are:

(1) The Horus Name: 𓅃 *hr*, often written over a rectangular frame, which represented, it is thought, the royal palace, and is called the 𓊹 *srh*—serekh. Horus was the falcon god who was the patron deity of the kings of Egypt. The kings were regarded as the living embodiment of the god upon earth and were often called 'the living Horus'.

(2) The Golden Horus Name: 𓅉 *hr nbw*. The derivation of this name is disputed. However, the monogram shows a falcon (Horus) standing on the hieroglyphic sign for gold, 𓋞 . It is possible that originally this name was 'the Horus and Seth Name', and that it was written 𓅃𓁗 , Horus and Seth being the patron deities of Lower and Upper Egypt respectively. Gradually, Seth fell out of favour, and became identified as Horus's enemy. Hence, the hieroglyph 𓁗 was replaced by 𓋞 , an abbreviation of 𓋞𓊖 *nbt* (Gold Town), the chief sanctuary of Seth: a more tactful way of associating Seth with Horus.

(3) The Nebty Name: 𓅐 𓆗 *nbty*. The term *nbty* means 'the Two Ladies' and refers to the goddesses Nekhbet and Edjo. Nekhbet was the vulture goddess who was

patron of Upper Egypt, whilst Edjo was the cobra goddess, patron of Lower Egypt. They were both embodiments of the crowns of their respective halves of the country—Nekhbet was identified with the White Crown of Upper Egypt (ⱱ) and Edjo with the Red Crown of Lower Egypt (ⱱ). The first king of a united Egypt, Menes, was probably the first to use the *nebty*-name, thus symbolizing the fact that he had united the Two Lands.

Part 2

PAPYRUS

In ancient times, the papyrus plant (*Cyperus papyrus L*) grew prolifically in the marshes of Egypt, especially in the Delta. From the Egyptian word for papyrus, ⱱ   *w3d*, was derived a myriad of meanings: green, fresh, fortunate, happy, flourish, and others. Unfortunately, thanks to the gradual silting up of the marshes which once lay between the desert edge and the cultivated land, and to attempts to reclaim and irrigate land, papyrus no longer grows naturally in Egypt.

The Egyptians used papyrus to make all manner of things—baskets, ropes, sandals, mats, clothes, boats. Above all, they used its triangular-shaped stem, which often grew to a height of 18 feet, to make a writing material: they cut the stem into pieces, freed the pith and sliced it, and then beat it with a hammer. Some of the wafer-thin strips thus arrived at were laid side-by-side on a board, and more strips were placed on top of them, at right angles to the lower layer. The two layers were then wetted, pressed firmly together and laid out to dry in the sun.

The length of stem cut from the original determined the height and width of a 'page', the standard size of which was some 20″ by 18″. Several pages were joined together into the desired length, which could then be rolled up—the standard papyrus roll consisted of twenty pages joined together—with the horizontal fibres on the inside. Both sides of a papyrus could be, and were, written on, but the side with the horizontal fibres was the preferred surface. The longest known papyrus roll is the Great Harris Papyrus (no. 9999 in the British Museum) which is just over 133′ in length.

The subject matter written on papyrus was various: administrative documents, accounts, medical and mathematical works, religious texts, and so on. Above all, the great works of literature were recorded on papyrus.

The script used on papyrus was often, as we saw in IEH (p. 39), *hieratic.* Just as handwriting today differs from person to person, with some having a good, clear hand-writing whilst others have one almost impossible to read, so each Egyptian scribe had his own 'hieratic hand'. Hence, difficulties are often experienced in reading hieratic.

The scholar normally attempts to *transcribe* a hieratic text into hieroglyphic script before transliterating and translating it. The following example, showing first part of a text in hieratic and then a transcription, will illustrate this; the hieratic text in this example is written *vertically*, from right to left, the hieroglyphic transcription is also written right to left.

Papyrus 1115, Leningrad Museum: The Story of the Shipwrecked Sailor
(dating to the Middle Kingdom)

EXERCISE 20(A)

Transliterate and translate the following:

1. [hieroglyphs]
   (Armant Stele of Tuthmosis III)

2. [hieroglyphs]
   (Gebel Barkal Stele of Tuthmosis III)

3. [hieroglyphs]
   (Amada Stele of Amenhotep II)

4. [hieroglyphs]
   (Inscription on Sehel Island, Aswan)

5. [hieroglyphs]

   . . .

   [hieroglyphs]

EXERCISE 20(B)

Copy out the hieroglyphic text of the Shipwrecked Sailor on page 152, horizontally, either from right to left or *vice versa* according to preference, and then transliterate and translate it, making philological notes on the text.

KEY TO EXERCISE 2

(a) 1. [hieroglyphs]

ỉn mr.f nb.f

2. [hieroglyphs]

ỉn b3k nfr mr.f nb.f r-ỉkr

3. [hieroglyphs]

wp sš r.f ỉḫ wšb.f n nsw

4. [hieroglyphs]

ỉst rf dỉ.ỉ t n ḥḳr r nb

5. [hieroglyphs]

nḏ-ḥrt.ỉ ỉs ḥm.f ḫft-ḥr n t3 r-ḏr.f

6. [hieroglyphs]

h3 nb.ỉ sḏm.ỉ ḥm n.k ḏt

(b) 1. Will you pass by this road tomorrow? (ỉn sw3.k ḥr w3t tn m-dw3(w))

2. Behold, this city is joyful (lit: in festival) today. (mk nỉwt tn m ḥb mỉn)

3. Now the overseer found the man at the gate of the palace. (gm grt ỉmy-r s ḥr sb3 n(y) pr-nsw)

4. Your wife is beautiful but you do not love her. (nfr ḥmt.k n mr.n.k swt sy)

KEY TO EXERCISE 3

(a) 1. [hieroglyphs]

'3 nṯr.ỉ nỉwty r nṯr.k nỉwty

2. [hieroglyphs]

pr ḥm-nṯr r ḥr(t)-nṯr ṯnw rnpt

3. [hieroglyphs]

dỉ.s n.f ḫt nbt nfrt

4. [hieroglyphs]

dr ḥry-tp ꜥ3 ḥryw-š̌ꜥ ḥry t3 pn

(b) 1. I love the god who is in the temple. (*mr.ỉ nṯr ỉmy r-pr*)

2. The beneficent king (or a beneficent king) gives every good thing to the whole land. (*dỉ nsw nfr ḫt nb(t) nfr(t) n t3 r-ḏr.f*)

3. Amun is mightier than all the gods of Egypt. (*nḫt ỉmn r nṯrw nb(w) n(w) kmt*)

4. The whole land rejoiced when it saw the god who is at the head of the ennead. (*rš̌ t3 r-3w.f m33.f nṯr ḫnty psḏt*)

5. His eldest daughter is the most beautiful of women. (*nfr s3t.f smsw.f ỉmy nfrwt*)

KEY TO EXERCISE 4

(a) 1. [hieroglyphs]

n-sy nb

2. [hieroglyphs]

š̌m nn n ḥmw r nỉwt r nb

3. [hieroglyphs]

dr nsw š̌m3 pf r t3wy

4. [hieroglyphs]

ꜥk š̌rỉt tn ḫft-ḥr nṯr nfr m p3 hrw

5. [hieroglyphs]

ḏd sy s nn

(b) 1. When (see IEH p. 103) the goddess speaks the whole land listens. (*ḏd t3 nṯrt sḏm t3 r-ḏr.f*)

2. I see the great boat which is on the water. (*m3.ỉ dpt wrt ḥryt mw*)

3. It belongs to the temple of the local god. (*n-sy r-pr n nṯr nỉwty*)

4. Anubis who is upon his mountain guards the necropolis. (*s3w ỉnpw tpy ḏw.f ḥr(t)-ntr*)

5. This splendid sun shines upon this noble land. (*wbn rꜥ pf ḥr t3 pw špss*)

KEY TO EXERCISE 5

(a) 1. 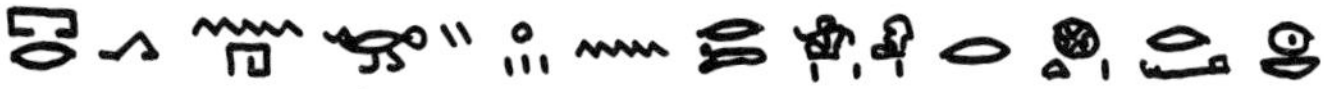 𓉐𓂻𓏏𓏤𓈖𓂋𓅓𓏏𓈖𓊖𓂋𓏤𓎟

   pr nhy n rmt r nỉwt rꜥ nb

2.  𓂋𓂝𓈖𓆑𓃀𓅱𓎟𓐍𓏏

   rdỉ n.f bw nb ḫt

3.  𓌡𓅓𓉗𓏤𓎟𓂋𓎡𓇌𓅓𓉐𓆑

   wꜥ m ḥwt-ntr ky m pr.f

4. 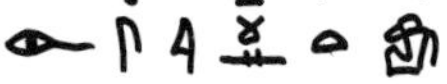 𓂋𓏤𓄿𓈙𓏏

   ỉr.s ỉšst

5.  �set𓂋𓂧𓎡𓂧𓋴𓎡𓈖𓈖

   ḏd.k ḏs.k nn

(b) 1. What am I doing? (*ỉr.ỉ m*)

2. The house is hers. (*nts p3 pr*)

3. She herself did not hear anyone. (*n sḏm.s ḏs.s. s*)

4. No one will give me bread. (*nn rdỉ n.ỉ s t*)

5. One kissed the other. (*wꜥt sn.s sn-nw.s*)

KEY TO EXERCISE 6

(a) 1. 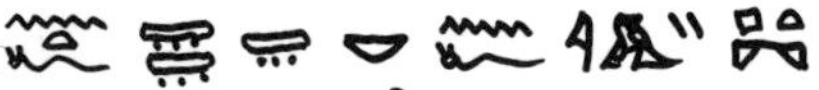 𓈖𓏏𓆑𓇾𓅱𓎟𓆑𓏌𓅓𓇯

   ntf t3w nb(w) n.f-ỉmy pt

2. 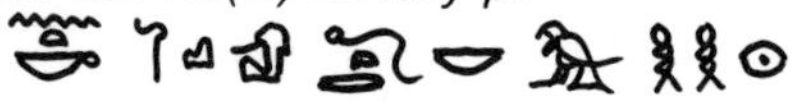 𓈖𓏏𓎡𓋾𓂧𓏏𓎟𓇳

   ntk ḥk3 ḏt nb nḥḥ

3. [hieroglyphs]

ỉw nn n ʿ3w n sn.ỉ or *n p3y.ỉ sn*

4. [hieroglyphs]

nn wn ḥbswt n wʿ m n3 n s

5. [hieroglyphs]

nn n.f mw or *nn wn mw.f*

(b) 1. To him belongs the sky and everything that is in it. (*ntf pt ḥnʿ ỉmyt.s nbt*)

2. Life is hers in this her city of eternity (i.e. her tomb). (*n.s-ỉmy ʿnḫ m nỉwt.s tn nt nḥḥ*)

3. This house, it belongs to me. (*pr pn n.ỉ-ỉmy sw*)

4. This property belongs to your children. (*ḫt tn n n3y.k n ḫrdw*)

5. She has no husband. (*nn wn hy.s*)

KEY TO EXERCISE 7

(a) 1. [hieroglyphs]

m3ʿt pw nb.n pw or

[hieroglyphs]

ỉw.s m m3ʿt ỉw.f m nb.n or

[hieroglyphs]

mk sy m m3ʿt . . . nb.n pw or *ỉw.f m nb.n*

2. [hieroglyphs]

ḥmt m ḥmt bỉnt nn st m pr n nb.s or

[hieroglyphs]

ḥmt m ḥmt bỉnt n ỉw.s m pr etc.

3. [hieroglyphs]

ỉw nn sš m pr.f

4. [hieroglyphs]

ỉnk šmsw n nb t3wy

5. 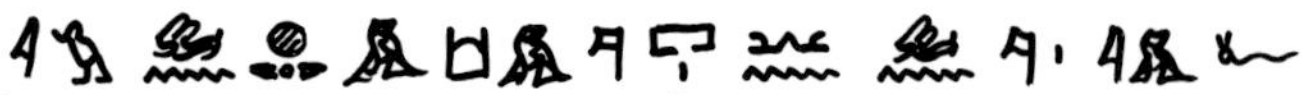 𓄿𓃾 𓈗 𓈘 𓉐𓊹𓏌𓇯 𓈗 𓈗𓏤 𓄿𓃾 ～

ỉw wn ḥm m pr-nṯr nn wn nṯr ỉm.f

(b) 1. Indeed, it is I who am the ruler of Punt. (*ỉnk ỉs ḥḳ3 pwnt*)

2. It is he in truth who is the heir of Osiris. (*ntf pw m m3ʿt ỉwʿ wsỉr ỉs pw*)

3. My father was a soldier in the palace. (*ỉw ỉt.ỉ m mšʿ m pr-nsw*)

4. It is better than anything. (*nfr st r ḫt nbt*)

5. She is in the house but he is not there. (*ỉw.s m pr nn sw ỉm*)

KEY TO EXERCISE 9

(a) 1.  𓉔𓂝𓃾𓂋𓏭𓆓 𓏏𓊪𓏏 𓂋 𓊖 𓏏𓆓 𓏭𓃾

h3b.ỉ dpt r nỉwt ḏ3.t(w).k ỉm.s

2. 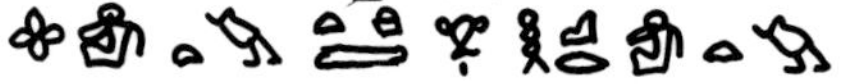 𓎸𓃀𓈖 𓏏𓏤 𓏏 𓏏𓇯 �...𓃀 𓈖

wnm tw t ḥr ḥḳr tw

3.  𓄤 𓐍𓅱𓆟 𓃀 𓊪𓃾 𓈖𓈖 𓈗 𓐍𓈖𓎡𓏏

nfr b3kw m swrỉ.sn ḥnḳt

4.  𓂋𓆳𓃾𓈙𓇳 𓇾 𓂋𓂧𓏤 𓂋 𓅓𓃾𓃾 𓈖𓏏𓂋𓅱 𓅓 𓋴𓏏𓈖 𓄤𓃾𓏌 𓈖𓏭𓏏 𓇋𓏠𓈖𓏏𓏏

ršw t3 r-ḏr.f ỉr m33 ntrw m swt.sn nfrwt nywt ỉmntt

5.  𓂋𓐍𓊃 𓈖𓈖 𓈖 𓏏𓆓𓏤 𓊪𓆑 𓏭𓐍𓃾 𓂋𓉐 𓊪𓈖

rḫ.s rn n nṯr pf ỉmy r-pr pn

(b) 1. When I see my daughter in my house, I am joyful (lit: in joy). (*m33.ỉ s3t.ỉ m pr.ỉ ỉw.ỉ m ršwt*)

2. Every heart is glad when the sun shines on the horizon. (*nfr ỉb nb ḫft wbn rʿ m 3ḫt*)

3. You tell it to your lord and he will tell (it) to his servant likewise.

or

If you tell it to your lord, then he will speak to his etc. (*ḏd.k st n nb.k ỉḫ ḏd.f n ḥm.f m mỉtt*)

4. His voice is heard in the temple by the priest. (*sḏm.tw ḫrw.f m r-pr ỉn ḥm-nṯr*)

5. Gifts have been brought so that they may be given to the king. (*ỉn.tw ỉnw rdỉ.tw.sn n nsw*)

KEY TO EXERCISE 10

(a) 1. [hieroglyphs]
rdỉw ḥkr t m nb.ỉ

2. [hieroglyphs]
ỉr.n.(ỉ) ḥwt-ntr tn n ỉt.ỉ ỉmn

3. [hieroglyphs]
spr.n.f r nỉwt n gm.f s nb

4. [hieroglyphs]
m3.n.s ḥm-ntr m-ḫt ꜥk.n.s r r-pr

5. [hieroglyphs]
rḫ.n nb.ỉ ỉnk ḥm nfr

(b) 1. If I had heard it, I would have given him gold. (*ỉr sdm.n.ỉ st ỉw rdỉ.n.ỉ n.f nbw*)
  2. He followed his lord when he was in (lit: upon) this foreign land. (*ỉw šms.n.f nb.f m wn.f ḥr ḫ3st tn*)
  3. I caused my image to be placed at the door of the temple. (*rdỉ.n.ỉ ỉr.tw twt.ỉ r sb3 ḥwt-ntr*)
  4. I went down to the Great Green (the Mediterranean) according as His Majesty commanded. (*h3.n.ỉ r w3d-wr ḫft wd.n ḥm.f*)
  5. It was reported to the Royal Herald and One gave me gold. (*smỉw n wḥmw-nsw rdỉ.n tw n.ỉ nbw*)

KEY TO EXERCISE 11

(a) 1. [hieroglyphs]
wšb ḥm.f n t3ty nn wšb.f n ḥmt tn

2.  𓉐𓀀𓂝 𓏥/𓉐𓀀𓂻 𓃂 𓏥 � 𓂝𓀀𓈖 𓃂 𓏤𓊹

ḫ3y (or ḫ3).ỉ r nỉwt m3n.ỉ pr-nṯr or

𓈖 𓂝𓀀 𓀭 𓏤𓊹

r m3n.ỉ pr-nṯr or

𓈖 𓋴𓏏𓂋 𓂝𓀀𓈖 𓀭 𓏤𓊹

n-mrwt m3n.ỉ pr-nṯr

3. 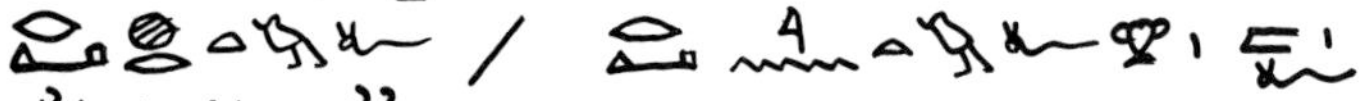 �2𓊖𓂝𓀀𓂻 / �2𓈖𓂝𓀀𓂻𓄿𓄹 𓍢

rdỉ.ḫr.tw.f (or rdỉ.ỉn.tw.f) ḥr gs.f

4.  � 𓈖 𓂝�I𓂝𓀀 𓈖 𓍢

rdỉ.n nṯr m3n.s ḥr.f

5.  𓃂𓀀𓀭𓂻 𓃀𓂝𓊨 𓀭𓃀𓂝 𓉐𓃀

ḫ3 ỉwt sn.ỉ r pr.ỉ

(b) 1. May the Inundation God bring him his offering, may he eat with his mouth. (*ỉnt n.f ḥp ḥtpt.f wnm.f m r.f*)

2. Then let us make a habitation together. (*ỉḫ ỉr.n dmỉ n-sp*)

3. O that he may act according as I say. (*ḥw ỉry.f ḫft ḏḏ.ỉ*)

4. His Majesty will cause his son to rise up in his place. (*rdỉ ḥm.f 'ḥ'w s3.f ḥr st.f*)

5. May I serve the Lady of the Universe so that she may tell me (of) the beauty of her children. (*šms.ỉ nbt r-ḏr ỉḫ ḏḏ.s n.ỉ nfrw msw.s*)

KEY TO EXERCISE 12

(a) 1.  𓉐𓀀𓂧𓂻 𓈖 𓈖𓂝𓊖 𓊨

ḫ3b n.f š't

2.  𓇋𓈖 𓂋𓂝 𓇋 �= 𓀀𓂻 𓈖 𓍢𓏤𓂝

ỉ' tw ỉmỉ mw ḥr db'w.k

3.  𓀀𓇋𓂻/𓀀𓂻 𓈖𓇋𓊗𓊪𓀀𓈙𓊖𓇳 𓂝 𓏏𓍢𓇋𓂝𓂻 𓈖 𓀭𓊹

mỉ r ḥwt-nṯr m hrw pn nfr ḏḏ ỉr.k n ḥm-nṯr

4.

ỉmỉ wỉ m-bȝḥ.k mȝ.ỉ ḥr.k

5.

ỉmỉ šm.n ḥr mtn pf

(b) 1. O Thoth, make Amenhotep triumphant! (ỉ ḏḥwty smȝ'-ḥrw ỉmnḥtp)

2. Pray come, my sister, so that I may speak to you. (mỉ my snt.ỉ mdw.ỉ n.t̠)

3. Equip for yourself a barque with beautiful women. ('pr n.k bȝw m nfrwt)

4. Go to him, let him learn your name. (hȝ n.f ỉmỉ rḫ.f rn.k)

5. Equip yourselves and make ready your weapons so that you may fight in the morning (or tomorrow). (grg ỉrf t̠n sspd ḫ'w.tn 'ḥȝ.t̠n m dwȝ)

KEY TO EXERCISE 13

(a) 1.

ḥmt.ỉ ḥr rnn sȝt.s šrỉt

2.

wḏ.n.f n.ỉ prt r ḥwt-nt̠r

3.

dw r tȝ m ḥtp ỉn mš' n nb tȝwy

4.

pḥrt nt smȝ ḫft

5.

nfr rdỉt r šsp

(b) 1. He was installed (rdỉ 'put') in order to hear disputes. (rdỉ.n.tw.f r sḏm mdwt)

2. Giving praise to Osiris, smelling the ground for Wepwawet by the count. (rdỉt ḥst n wsỉr sn-tȝ n wp-wȝwt ỉn ḥȝty-')

3. A book for driving out all snakes. (šfdw n dr ḥfȝw nb)

4. To do justice is the breath of the nose. (t̠ȝw pw n fnd ỉrt mȝ't)

5. His Majesty commanded that the offerings be doubled (i.e. commanded to double the offerings) when His Majesty returned from subduing Rethenu. (*ỉw wḏ.n ḥm.f kb ḥtpw-nṯr m-ḫt ỉỉt ḥm.f ḥr dr ṯnw*)

KEY TO EXERCISE 14

(a) 1. [hieroglyphs]
ḥmt wꜥb pw n rꜥ ỉwr.tỉ m ḥrdw 3

2. [hieroglyphs]
ỉỉ.n nsw ḥr wꜥrt bꜣk.tỉ m nbw

3. [hieroglyphs]
gm.n.f ḥm-nṯr ḥms(w) m r-pr

4. [hieroglyphs]
rdỉ.kwỉ r pr sꜣ-nsw

5. [hieroglyphs]
ḏd.tw n.f ỉỉ.tỉ m ḥtp ỉn nṯrw nb

(b) 1. We knew that she was a goddess because she spoke these words. (*rḫ.wyn nṯrt pw ḏd.n.s nn n mdwt*)

2. Then His Majesty sailed downstream, his heart being glad. (*nꜥt m ḫd ỉn ḥm.f ỉb.f ꜣw*)

3. I went down to the mining region. (*šm.kwỉ r bỉꜣ*)

4. A splendid harp worked with silver and gold. (*bnt špst bꜣk.tỉ m ḥḏ nbw*)

5. No man spent the night hungry in my town. (*n sḏr s ḥkrw r dmỉ.ỉ*)

KEY TO EXERCISE 15

(a) 1. [hieroglyphs]
ỉw dpt r ỉỉt m kmt

2.

rdi̯.n.i̯ wi̯ ḥr ḫt.i̯ ʿwy.i̯ ḫ3m m b3ḥ.f

3.

mk tw r spr r kmt n 3bd 2

4.

mk wi̯ i̯i̯.kwi̯ r ḥmst m pr pn

5.

ḥm.f ḥr ḫntyt i̯b.f 3w

(b) 1. Behold you will spend month after month on (lit: in) this island. (*mk tw r i̯rt 3bd ḥr 3bd m-ḫnw n i̯w pn*)

2. Now His Majesty spent his time seeking these chambers. (*i̯st wrš ḥm.f ḥr ḫḥy n3 n i̯pwt*)

3. I controlled all work, my opinion (lit: heart) being useful to His Majesty. (*i̯w.i̯ ḥr ḫrp k3t nbt i̯b.i̯ 3ḫ(w) n ḥm.f*)

4. Behold, I am come to you. (*mk wi̯ i̯i̯.kwi̯ n.k*)

5. Every man seizes the property of his fellow. (*s nb ḥr i̯tt ḫt snnw.fy*)

KEY TO EXERCISE 16

wn.ḥr.i̯ ḥr šms   i̯ty   ʿnḫ wḏ3   snb   ḥr rdwy.i̯ m-ḫt swtwt.f
Then I accompanied the sovereign, life, prosperity, health, on foot when he rode abroad
ḥr wrr(y)t.f   i̯w ḥms.tw   ḥr dmi̯ n ḥwt-wʿrt wn.ḥr.i̯ ḥr ḳnt   ḥr rdwy.i̯ m-b3ḥ
in his chariot. One besieged the city of Avaris; and then I showed valour on foot before
ḥm.f   ʿḥ'.n.i̯   dhn-kwi̯   r ḫʿ-m-mn-nfr   wn.i̯.tw ḥr
His Majesty. Thereupon I was promoted to (the ship) 'Shining in Memphis'. Then One
ʿḥ3   ḥr mw   m   p3   ḏdkw   n ḥwt-wʿrt ʿḥ'.n ḫf'.n.i̯
fought on the water, it being the (canal named) Djedeku of Avaris. Thereupon I made a
i̯n.i̯   drt   smi̯.t(w)   n wḥmw-nsw   wn.i̯n.tw ḥr rdi̯t n.i̯ nbw
capture and brought away a hand. It was reported to the Royal Herald. One gave me the

n knt   ʿḥʿ n wḥmw ʿḥ3   m st tn   wn.ỉn.ỉ ḥr wḥm ḫfʿ   ỉm

gold of valour. Then there was fighting again in this place. Again, I made a capture there

ỉn.ỉ   drt   wn.ỉn.tw ḥr rdỉt n.ỉ nbw n knt   m wḥm-ʿ wn.ỉn.tw ḥr ʿḥ3 m t3 kmt

and brought away a hand. One gave me the gold of valour again. One fought in Egypt

rsyt   n dmỉ pn   ʿḥʿ.n   ỉn.n.ỉ   skrỉ-ʿnḫ   s   ḥ3.n.ỉ   r   p3

south of this city. Then I brought away a living captive, a man, and went down to the

mw   mk (= ḥr) ỉntw.f m mḥ   ḥr   t3   w3t   p3 dmỉ ḏ3.n.ỉ   ḥr.f   ḥr

water, bringing him as a captive upon the road of the city. I crossed with him over the

mw   smỉw   n   wḥmw.nsw   ʿḥʿ.n.tw mk (= ḥr) ỉwʿ.ỉ m nbw ḥr snnw.sy wn.

water. It was reported to the Royal Herald. One rewarded me with gold yet again. One

ỉn.tw ḥr ḥ3k ḥwt-wʿrt wn.ỉn.ỉ ḥr ỉnt ḥ3kwt ỉm   s 1   st-ḥmt 3   dmḏ-r tp 4

sacked Avaris. Then I brought away plunder thence: 1 man, 3 women, total—4 people.

KEY TO EXERCISE 17

(a) 1.
nfrwy nsw ḫnty mšʿ.f

2.
m3.n.f sb3 sʿḥʿ.tw thnwy b3k(w) m ḏ'mw m-ḥ3t.f

3.
bw wršw ỉb.ỉ ỉm

4.
ỉ sšw ʿkty.sn r ỉs pn m33ty.sn ntt ỉm.f

5.
ỉt.n.ỉ ntt nbt m dmỉ.f

(b) 1. Osiris, to whom was given the rule in Heliopolis. (*wsỉr rdy.n.f ḥḳ3t m ỉwnw*)

2. How happy is he whom his father has taught. (*nfrwy sb3.n ỉt.f*)

3. These things which I have given to these priests in exchange for these things which they have given to me. (*nn n ḫt rdỉ.nỉ n nn n wʻbw m-ỉsw nn n ḫt rdỉ.n.sn nỉ*)

4. Moreover, as for any son of mine who shall maintain this boundary. (*ỉr grt s3ỉ nb srwd(y).fy t3š pn*)

5. O ye who sit in the prow (lit: in the front (*ḥ3t*) of) the barque of Re, who ever give offerings to the gods. (*ỉ ḥmsyw m ḥ3t wỉ3 n rʻ dd ḥtpw-nṯr n nṯrw*)

KEY TO EXERCISE 18

(a) 1.

ḫbswt.f wr s(y) r mḥ 2

2.

ỉn nb.ỉ h3b nbw ntk dd n.ỉ st

3.

ỉn ḥmt ddt n.f st

4.

prr ḥm-nṯr r r-pr ḥr-m

5.

dd.tw nn n ḫt n s3.ỉ

(b) 1. It is in his name that you shall cause the oath to be established. (*ỉḫ dd.k mn.tw ʻnḫ m rn.f*)

2. It is as he wishes that His Majesty will act. (*ỉrr ḥm.f m mrt.f*)

3. It is I who am the ruler of Punt. (*ỉnk ỉs ḥḳ3 pwnt*)

4. That oil which you spoke of bringing, it is the principal product of this island. (*ḥknw pf ḏd.n.k ỉnt.f bw pw wr n ỉw pn*)

KEY TO EXERCISE 19

(a) 1. [hieroglyphs]

nn 3tpw pw ḥr-'wy.k

2. [hieroglyphs]

n sp îr.tw mîtt dr p3wt

3. [hieroglyphs]

tm.k sdm n.î ḥr-m

4. [hieroglyphs]

m 'wn ḥwrw ḥr ḫt.f

5. [hieroglyphs]

nn wn nḥm.n.î ḫt.f

(b) 1. I shall not mention to you a daughter who was brought to me by god. (*nn sḫ3.î n.k s3t înt n.î m nṯr*)

2. Spell for not allowing the heart to create opposition. (*r n tm rdît sḫsf îb*)

3. Do not let these evil words be said. (*m rdî dd.tw nn n mdwt dwwt*)

4. He who shall hear this shall not say (that) what I have said is boasting. (*nn dd sdmty.fy nn 'b' pw ddt.n.î*)

5. She whom he had never seen is (now) possessor of his property. (*îw tmt.n.f m33 m nbt ḫt.f*)

KEY TO EXERCISE 20(A)

1. *ḥ3t sp 22 3bd 2 prt sw 10*

   Regnal year 22 month 2 of peret day 10.

2. *ḥ3t sp 47 3bd 3 3ḫt sw 10*

   Regnal year 47 month 3 of Inundation day 10.

3. *ḥ3t sp 3 3bd 3 šmw sw 15*

   Regnal year 3 month 3 of Summer day 15.

4. *ḥ3t sp 50 tpy (n) šmw sw 22 ḥr ḥm n nsw b*̣*t (mn-ḫpr-r') d*̣ *'nḫ*

   Regnal year 50 first month of Summer day 22 under the Majesty of the King of Upper and Lower Egypt (Menkheperre) given life.

5.(a) *'nḫ   ḥr   nṯr   ḫprw*

   Long live the Horus divine of forms

   (b) *nbty   nṯr   mswt*

   The Two Ladies divine of births

   (c) *nsw b*̣*t   (ḫ'-k3w-r')   d*̣ *'nḫ*

   The King of Upper and Lower Egypt (Kha-kau-Re) given life

   (d) *'nḫ   ḥr nbw   ḫpr   s3 r' n ḫt.f*

   Long live the Golden Horus who has come into being, the bodily son of Re,

   (e) *mr.f   nb t3wy   (s-n-wsrt)   d*̣ *'nḫ*

   his beloved, the Lord of the Two Lands (Sesostris) given life,

   (f) *dd   w3s   dt*

   stability and dominion forever.

   (g) *ḥ3t sp 16   3bd 3   prt   ṣrt ḥm.f*

   Regnal year 16 month 3 of Winter: His Majesty's making of the

   (h) *t3š rsy   r   ḥḥ*

   southern boundary at Heh.

   (i) *t3š rsy   ṣry   m   ḥ3t sp 8   ḥr   ḥm*

   The southern boundary which was fixed in Year 8 under the Majesty

   (j) *n   nsw-b*̣*t   (ḫ'-k3w-r')   d*̣ *'nḫ*

   of the King of Upper and Lower Egypt (Kha-kau-Re) given life

   (k) *dt r nḥḥ   r   tm rd*̣*.sn sw nḥsy nb*

   for ever and ever, in order to prevent any Nubian passing it

   (l) *m ḫd   m ḥrt   m k3*̣

   when faring northwards either by land or by boat.

Philological notes to no. 5

line (a): *'nḫ ḥr—sdm.f* with noun subject (Horus) in optative mood; *'long* live' is a 'free' translation.

　　　　 nṯr(w) —stative, 3rd person sing. masc. describing Horus.

line (b): *nṯr(tï)*—stative, 3rd person plural describing Two Ladies

line (c): *dï 'nḫ*—common abbreviation of *rdy 'nḫ.f* 'may it be given (*rdy*—prospective *sḏm.f* with unstated subject) that he live.'

line (d): *ḫpr* —imperfective active participle, masc. to agree with *ḥr*.

line (g): *ïrt* —infinitive.

line (i): *ïry* —perfective passive participle, masc. to agree with *t3š*.

line (k): *r tm* —negative verb *tm* in subordinate clause after preposition *r*.

line (l): *m ḫd* —pseudo-verbal construction employing *m* plus infinitive with verb of motion.

KEY TO EXERCISE 20(B)

The Shipwrecked Sailor is describing a snake that he met after he had been cast up on a desert island . . . 'he was 30 cubits long, his beard was over 3 cubits long, his limbs were overlaid with gold' . . .

line

65 *m nbw   ïn(h)wy.fy   m   ḥsbd*

with gold, his eyebrows were real lapis lazuli.

66 *m3'   'rḳ sw r ḫnt*

He was rearing up (lit: raised up he was in front).

67 *ïw wp.n.f r.f   r.ï   ïw.ï*

He opened his mouth to me, I being

68 *ḥr ḥt.ï   m b3ḥ.f*

on my belly in front of him.

69 *ḏd.f   n.ï   (ï)n-m   ïn.tw   sp 2   nḏs*

He said to me, "Who has brought you, who has brought you, little man?"

70   *(i̯)n-m*   *i̯n*   *tw*   *i̯r wdf.*

Who has brought you? If you delay

71   *k m ḏd*   *n.i̯*   *i̯n tw*   *r*   *i̯w pn*

in telling me who has brought you to this island

72   *rdi̯.i̯*   *rḫ.k*   *tw*   *i̯w.k*   *m*   *ss*

I will cause you to know yourself, you being as ashes

73   *ḫpr.t(i̯)*   *m*   *nty*   *n*   *m3.t(w).f*   *i̯w mdw.*

having become as one who is no longer (lit: not) seen!" "You speak

74   *k n.i̯*   *nn wi̯*   *ḥr sḏm*

to me but I do not understand

75   *st*   *i̯w.i̯ m b3ḫ.k*

(it). Because I am in your presence

76   *ḫmn wi̯*   *ʿḥ ʿ.n rdi̯.f wi̯*

I have lost my wits (lit: I do not know myself)!" Then he placed me

77   *m r.f*   *i̯t.f*   *wi̯*   *r st.f*

in his mouth and carried me to his

78   *nt snḏm*   *w3ḫ*

resting place and set

79   *wi̯*   *nn*   *dmi̯t.i̯*   *wḏ3*

me down, nothing having touched me. . . .

Philological notes

line 69: Note that hieroglyphic script does not have any way of indicating the opening of inverted commas.

    🔣 = 🔣 *ỉn m* 'who?'

    🔣 *sp sn*, lit: two times, indicates that preceding phrase should be repeated.

line 73: *ḫpr.t(ỉ)*—stative 2nd person sing., masc. *nty n m3.t(w).f*—relative adjective *nty* followed by negation of a *sḏm.tw.f.*

line 74/5: *nn wỉ ḥr sḏm st*—*ḥr* plus infinitive qualifying preceding dependent pronoun (*wỉ*); note that Egyptian must express object (*st*) where English does not.

line 78: *nt snḏm*—*nt* is feminine genitival adjective to agree with *st.*

line 79: *dmỉt* is *not* a feminine infinitive in spite of the *t*. Verbs such as 🔣 *dmỉ* 'touch' and 🔣 *smỉ* 'report' employ the hieroglyph 🔣 which seems originally to have had the value *mr* rather than *mỉ*. Hence, *dmỉ* and *smỉ* are treated as though they were spelled *dmr, smr,* and as strong verbs they have masculine infinitives. In Line 79, *dmỉt.ỉ* is the feminine/neuter relative form; *nn dmỉt.ỉ,* literally, is 'there did not exist that which had touched me' (see p. 128, B6, iii).

ENGLISH-EGYPTIAN VOCABULARY

A

after 𓂝𓐍𓏏 *m-ḫt*

all 𓎟 *nb*

allow 𓂋𓂡 *rdỉ*, followed by a *sḏm.f*

always 𓆓𓏏 *ḏt*

Amun 𓇋𓏠𓈖𓀭 *ỉmn*

answer 𓄿𓂋𓏤 × 𓅱 *wšb*

arm 𓂝 ‘

army 𓀀, 𓀀 *mš‘*

arrive 𓊪𓂋 *spr, r* at

ass 𓂝𓃘 *‘3*

assuredly �𓏤 *ḥm*

B

bad 𓃀𓇋𓈖𓅪 *bỉn*

beard 𓆓𓏤𓄞𓀀 *ḫbswt*

beautiful 𓄤𓆑𓂋 *nfr*

beduin 𓌔𓄿𓈙 *ḫryw-š‘*

beer 𓏐𓇋𓏊 *ḥnḳt*

before 𓂝𓄤𓏏 *m-ḥ3t*

behold 𓇋𓊃𓏏 *ỉst*, 𓐝𓏤, 𓐝𓂝 *mk*

belly 𓄡𓏏 *ẖt*

better: comparative of 𓄤𓆑𓂋 *nfr* good

boat 𓊞𓊛 *dpt*

bread 𓏏𓄹 *t*

brother 𓂊𓋴𓈖 *sn*

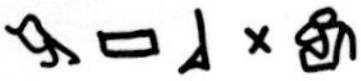

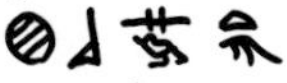

burden 𓄪𓎟𓅱𓀢 *3tpw*

by 𓈖 *ỉn*

C

cast 𓂞𓂡 *rdỉ*

chariot 𓍯𓎡𓅱 *wrrt*

chief 𓏲𓂧 *ḥry-tp*

child 𓀔 *ḥrd*

city 𓊖 *nỉwt*

come 𓇌𓂻 *ỉỉ*; 𓂻𓅱 *ỉw*

command 𓏏𓅱𓂡 *wḏ*

cubit 𓂭 *mḥ*

D

daily 𓂋𓎼 *r' nb*

day 𓉔𓂋𓅱𓇳 *hrw*; every day 𓂋𓎼 *r' nb*

daughter 𓅭𓄿 , 𓅭𓄿𓁐 *s3t*

defraud 𓋴𓈖𓀢 *'wn* plus *ḥr*

despatch 𓍿𓏏 *š't*

do 𓁹 *ỉrỉ*

drink 𓃀𓈎𓇋𓈗𓀢 *swrỉ*

drive away,—out 𓂧𓀢 *dr*

E

eat 𓃟𓀢 *wnm*

Egypt 𓆎𓅓𓏏𓊖 *kmt*

electrum 𓈖𓃀𓊪𓏤 *ḏ'mw*

enter 𓂝𓎡 *'k, r* into

entire 𓂋𓇥𓂋 *r-ḏr*

erect 𓋴𓉺𓂝 *s'ḥ'*

eternity 𓆓𓏏 *ḏt*

every ⬮ *nb*

everyone 𓂋𓏤𓂜𓁐𓏥 *bw nb*

everlasting 𓋹𓈖𓎛𓎛𓇳 *nḥḥ*

exceedingly ⬮𓏤𓄿𓏥 *r-ꜣkr*

F

face 𓁷𓏤 *ḥr*

father 𓇋𓏏𓀀 *ꞽt*

ferry across 𓂝𓊡𓈋 *ḏꜣꞽ*

few 𓈖𓄙𓏏𓏭𓏥 *nhy*

find 𓅠𓅓𓏏 *gmꞽ*

finger 𓂍𓏤 *ḏbꜥ*

fold 𓇉𓄿𓅓 *ḫꜣm*

follower 𓌞𓋴𓅱 *šmsw*

foreigner �𓈋𓀒 *šmꜣ*

G

gate 𓊨 *sbꜣ*

girl 𓋴𓂋𓇋𓏏 *šrꞽt*

give 𓂞𓏏 ; varr. 𓂞 , 𓂞𓏏 *dꞽ*

go 𓉐𓂻 *prꞽ*, 𓈝𓅓𓂻 *šm, r* to; go down 𓉔𓈎𓂻 *hꜣꞽ*; go up 𓉐𓂻 *prꞽ*, with *r*

god 𓊹𓏤 , 𓊹𓏏𓂋 *nṯr*

gold 𓋞 *nbw*

good 𓄤 , 𓄤𓆑𓂋 *nfr*

great 𓉻𓄿 *ꜥꜣ*

greet 𓈖𓆓𓊵𓂝𓏏𓏥 *nḏ-ḫrt*

H

happy 𓄤 , 𓄤𓆑𓂋 *nfr*

he 𓆑 *f* (suffix-pro.); 𓈖𓏏𓆑 *ntf* (indep. pro.); 𓇓𓅱 *sw* (dep. pro.); 𓊪𓅱 *pw* (demonst. pro.)

head, at the—of ⟨hieroglyphs⟩ ḫnty

heart ⟨hieroglyph⟩ ỉb

heaven ⟨hieroglyph⟩ pt

her ⟨hieroglyph⟩ s (suffix-pro.); ⟨hieroglyph⟩ nts (indep. pro.) ⟨hieroglyph⟩ sy (dep. pro.)

him ⟨hieroglyph⟩ f (suffix-pro.); ⟨hieroglyph⟩ ntf (indep. pro.)

his ⟨hieroglyph⟩ f (suffix-pro.)

house ⟨hieroglyph⟩ , ⟨hieroglyph⟩ pr

hungry, be ⟨hieroglyphs⟩ ḥḳr; hungry man ⟨hieroglyphs⟩ ḥḳr

I

I ⟨hieroglyph⟩ (suffix-pro.); ⟨hieroglyphs⟩ ỉnk (indep. pro.); ⟨hieroglyphs⟩ wỉ (dep. pro.)
⟨hieroglyphs⟩ kwỉ (Stative)

in ⟨hieroglyph⟩ m, ỉm before suffixes

indeed ⟨hieroglyph⟩ ỉs

it ⟨hieroglyph⟩ s (suffix-pro.); ⟨hieroglyph⟩ sy (dep. pro.); ⟨hieroglyph⟩ pw (demonst. pro.)

J

joyful ⟨hieroglyphs⟩ 3w ỉb (lit: long of heart)

K

king ⟨hieroglyphs⟩ nsw

king's son ⟨hieroglyphs⟩ s3-nsw

know ⟨hieroglyphs⟩ rḫ

L

land (noun) ⟨hieroglyph⟩ t3; (verb) ⟨hieroglyphs⟩ dw r t3

like ⟨hieroglyphs⟩ mỉtt

listen ⟨hieroglyphs⟩ sḏm

little ⟨hieroglyphs⟩ šrỉ

local ⟨hieroglyph⟩ nỉwty

long ⟨hieroglyph⟩ wr

lord ⬭ , ⬭, ⬭ 𓏞 *nb*
love (noun) 𓄟𓄿𓏞 *mrwt*; (verb) 𓄟𓏞 *mrı͗*

M

majesty 𓈏 *ḥm*
make ⬭ *ı͗rı͗*
man 𓀀 *s*
master ⬭ , ⬭ 𓏞 *nb*
me 𓅱𓏞 *wı͗* (dep. pro.)
month ⬭ 𓇹 *3bd*
mouth ⬭ *r*
my 𓏞 *ı͗* (suffix-pro.)

N

name 𓂋𓈖 *rn*
necropolis 𓄿 𓊨 𓈗 *ẖr(t)-nṯr*
no-one 𓀀 ⬭ *s nb*
nurse 𓈗 𓅱 *rnn*

O

O (vocative) 𓇋𓏞 *ı͗*, 𓉔𓅡 *h3*
obelisk 𓂝𓏤 𓊵 *tẖn*
obey 𓄑𓊃 ⬭ *sḏm n*
on 𓏠 *ḥr*, 𓊪 with suffixes
one ⬭ *w'*; (pronoun) 𓂝𓅱 *tw*; one . . . other 𓎼 𓏤 . . . ⬭𓏥 *w' . . . ky*
open 𓂧𓏴 *wpı͗*

P

peace 𓊵𓏏𓊪 *ḥtp*
place (noun) 𓃀𓅱 *bw*; 𓊨𓏏 *st*; (verb) 𓂞 *rdı͗*
poor man 𓀁𓄟𓅱𓀀 *ḥwrw*

possessions 𓄹𓏛 *ḫt*

pregnant 𓄿𓄿𓄹 *iwr*

presence, in the—of 𓄹𓇳𓈖 *ḥft-ḥr n;* 𓄹𓏤 , 𓄹𓃀𓄹𓄹𓏤 *m-bꜣḥ*

priest 𓃀𓈗𓊹 *wꜥb;* 𓍿𓃀 , 𓍿𓃀𓊹 , 𓍿𓃀𓊹 , *ḥm-nṯr*

primaeval times 𓄿𓊖 *pꜣwt*

proceed 𓈝𓄿𓂻 *šm;* var. 𓈝

put 𓂋 *rdi*

R

Re 𓂋𓇳𓏭 *rꜥ*

receive 𓄣𓃂 *šsp*

rejoice 𓇼𓇯𓏲 *ršw*

remedy 𓄤𓂝𓏥 *pḫrt*

road 𓈖𓏤𓊃𓈗 *mtn*

ruler 𓋹𓂓𓏥 *ḥkꜣ*

S

sail southwards/upstream 𓈗𓈗𓈗𓈗𓈖𓊖 *ḫnti* (infin: 𓈗𓈗𓈗𓈗𓈖𓂻𓊖 *ḫntyt*)

say 𓆓𓂧 *ḏd*

scribe 𓏞𓅱𓊹 *sš*

see 𓌳𓄿𓄿 *mꜣꜣ*

seize 𓄿𓂝𓈗𓏏 𓂡

self (yourself, etc.—see General Index under Reflexive)

send 𓉔𓄿𓂻 *hꜣb*

servant 𓅡𓂝𓊹 *bꜣk;* 𓍿𓏤 , 𓍿𓊹 *ḥm*

she 𓊃 *s* (suffix-pro.); 𓊪𓅱 *pw* (demonst. pro.)

ship 𓊞𓂧 *dpt*

shrine 𓄤𓄿𓉐 *ḥm*

side 𓎼𓏤 *gs*

since 𓂦 *ḏr*

sit 𓅆 𓀆 *ḥmsỉ*
slay 𓏤𓄿𓀒𓂧 *sm3*
something 𓏠𓏥 *ḫt*
so that 𓂋 *r;* 𓈖𓏥𓅆 *n-mrwt*
speak 𓆓 *ḏd*
spend the day 𓅢𓂋𓆄𓇳 *wršw*

T

take away 𓈖𓄿𓅓 *nḥm*
temple 𓉐𓊹 *pr-nṯr;* 𓂋𓊹 *r-pr;* 𓉐 , 𓉐𓏤 *ḥwt-nṯr*
that 𓊪𓆑 *pf*
their 𓊪𓏥 *sn* (suffix-pro.)
these 𓐍𓐍 *nn*
they 𓊪𓏥 *sn* (suffix-pro.)
thing 𓏠𓈖 *ḫt*
this 𓊪𓈖 *pn;* 𓏏𓈖 *tn;* 𓐍𓐍 *nn*
to 𓈖 *n;* 𓂋 *r*
today 𓅓𓊪𓆄𓇳 *m p3 hrw* (lit: on this day)
tomb 𓇋𓊃 *ỉs*
town 𓊖 *nỉwt*
truth 𓐙𓏏 *m3't*
Two Lands (Egypt) 𓇾𓇾 , 𓇾𓇾 *t3wy*

U

upon 𓁷 *ḥr,* with suffixes 𓁹
us 𓈖𓏥 *n* (suffix-pro.)

V

vile 𓊪𓆑 *pf* (see page 21)
vizier 𓍿𓇋𓏏 *ṯ3ty*

W

wash   𓇋𓈗𓂝 *ỉwʿ*

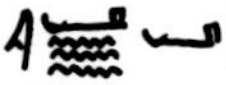

water   𓈗 *mw*

welcome   𓇋𓇋𓎛𓏏𓇋 *ỉỉ.tỉ*

west   𓋀𓏏𓏏 *ỉmntt*

what?   𓇋𓐠𓏏𓏥 *ỉšst*

whole   𓂋𓇥𓂋 *r-ḏr (f)*; see page 17

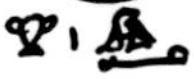

why?   𓁷𓂋𓅓 *ḥr-m*

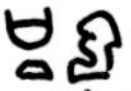

wife   �𓈟 *ḥmt*

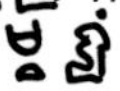

woman   𓈟 *ḥmt*; 𓋴𓏏 *st*

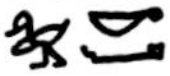

work   𓃀𓎡 *b3k*

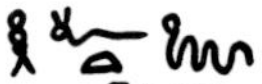

worm   𓆑𓏏 *ḥft*

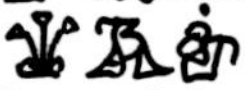

would that   𓉔𓍿 *ḥ3*

wrought   𓃀𓎡𓏏𓇋 *b3k.tỉ* (3rd person Stative of 𓃀𓎡 to work)

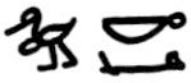

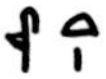

Y

year   𓆳 *rnpt*

you   𓎡 *k* (suffix-pro.); 𓈖𓏏𓎡 *ntk* (indep. pro.); 𓏏𓅱 , 𓏏𓅱 *tw* (dep. pro.)

your   𓎡 *k* (suffix-pro.)

yourself—see General Index under Reflexive

EGYPTIAN-ENGLISH VOCABULARY

3

𓄿 *3w* long; *r 3w(.f)* all, entire; 𓄿 *3w ỉb* joyful

𓇺, *3bd* month

3ḫ useful

3ḥt inundation

3ḫt horizon

ỉ

ỉ I, my

ỉ O! (vocative)

ỉỉ return

ỉw island

ỉw see General Index under Auxiliary Verbs; Pseudo-verbal Construction

ỉwꜥ heir

ỉwꜥ reward

ỉwnw Heliopolis

ỉb heart, mind, opinion

ỉpt chamber

ỉm there, therefrom, thence

ỉmỉ Imperative of *rdỉ* give

ỉmy who is in (*nisbe* adjective)

ỉmy-r overseer

ỉmn Amun

ỉmn-ḥtp Amenhotep

ỉn by; indeed; interrogative particle

ỉn , *ỉn* formative element in auxiliary verb *wn.ỉn*

ỉnỉ bring, bring away

𓂚𓈖𓏛𓏥 *ỉnw* gifts

𓇋𓈖𓊪𓅱𓃢 *ỉnpw* Anubis

𓇋𓄹𓏤 *ỉn(ḥ)wy* eyebrows

𓏞𓊪 *ỉnk* I

𓇋𓂋 *ỉr* if; 𓇋𓂋 𓎼𓏏 *ỉr grt* moreover

𓁹 *ỉrỉ* do; make; act; place; spend (time)

𓇋𓐍 *ỉḫ* so that, then; particle

𓇋𓊃 *ỉs* indeed, particle

𓌱𓈘𓏤 *ỉsw: m ỉsw* in exchange for

𓇋𓊨𓏤 *ỉst* now

𓇋𓏏𓅑 *ỉt* father

𓇋𓃰𓏤𓏤𓅆 *ỉty* sovereign

𓂡𓏏𓂻 *ỉtỉ* seize

ꜥ

𓂝𓃀𓏤𓀁 *ꜥb* boasting

𓂡𓊪𓂋 *ꜥpr* equip

𓋹𓈖𓐍 *ꜥnḫ* life; 'long live'

𓋹𓈖𓐍𓅪 *ꜥnḫ* oath

𓂝𓂋𓈎𓏤 *ꜥrḳ* raised up, bent

�ꜥ𓄿𓏤 , 𓂝𓄿𓂻 *ꜥḥꜣ* fight

𓊢𓂝𓏤 *ꜥḥꜥ* see under Auxiliary Verbs

𓊢𓂝𓀀 *ꜥḥꜥ* rise up

w

𓅱𓄿𓎛𓏲𓏭𓂻 *wꜣḥ* set down

𓅱𓄿𓏏𓈖 , 𓈅 , *wꜣt* road

𓇅𓇳𓅱𓂋 *wꜣḏ-wr* the Great Green (Mediterranean)

𓅱𓇋𓄿𓊛 *wỉꜣ* barque, boat

𓏺𓏤 *wꜥ* one

𓈖𓃀𓅆 *wꜥb* priest

𓅱 *wy* particle denoting admiration: How . . .!

𓅱𓈖 *wyn* we

𓅱𓈖𓇳 *wbn* shine

𓎛𓏴 *wp* open

𓎛𓏤𓃂 *wp-w3wt* Wepwawet

𓃹𓈖 *wn* exist

𓃹𓈖 , 𓃹 *wn* see under Auxiliary Verbs

𓎝𓀁 *wnm* eat

𓅨 *wr* great

𓅨𓏤𓄿 *wrr(y)t* chariot

𓅨𓎶𓇳 *wrš* spend time

𓊧 *wḥm* repeat

𓊧𓂝 *wḥm-ʿ: m wḥm-ʿ* again

𓊧 *wḥmw* repeat; 𓂝𓊧 *wḥmw-nsw* royal herald

𓊨𓁹 *wsἰr* Osiris

𓅨𓊃 *wsrt* the Strong One

𓅨𓂋𓆑 *wdf* delay

𓏏𓎛 *wḏ* command

𓎝 *wḏ3* prosperity

b

𓃀𓆓𓄿𓊛 *b3w* barque

𓃀𓆓𓀀𓐍 *b3ḫ: m b3ḫ* in front of

𓆓𓎸 *b3k* work

𓃀𓃀𓎶 *bἰ3* mining region

𓃀𓅨 *bw: bw wr* principal product

𓃀𓈖𓐠 *bnt* harp

p

𓅮 *p3* the

𓊪𓅱 *pw* see under Non-verbal sentences

□ 𓂝 𓈖 𓈎 *pwnt* Punt

𓀀 *pf* this, that

𓈖 *pn* this (m.)

𓉐 *pr* house

𓊪𓉐, 𓊪𓈖𓉐, *pr-nsw* palace

𓉐𓇳 *prt* winter

𓊪𓂧 *psḏt* ennead (group of nine gods)

𓊪𓏏 *pt* sky

f

𓆑 *f* he, him, his (suffix-pronoun)

𓆑𓂧𓏤 *fnd* nose

m

𓅓 *m* in, with; negative word

𓅓 *m* what?

𓅓 *(in)-m* who?

𓂝 *m* in, with etc.

𓐝𓅓 *m33* see

𓐝 𓏛 *m3ʿ* real

𓐝 𓏛, 𓐝 𓏛 *m3ʿt* justice, truth

𓅓𓂋 *mi* come (Imperative)

𓅓𓇳 *min* today

𓅓𓇳𓏛 *mitt* likewise

𓅓 *my* prithee, pray

𓈗 *mw* water

𓂝𓎛 *m-b3ḥ* before, in the presence of

𓏠𓏛 *mn* establish

𓏠 𓄤 *mn-nfr* Memphis (lit: 'Abiding and Beautiful', epithet of the pyramid that gave its name to the city)

𓐝 𓂋, *mri* love

mrt will, wish, desire

mḥ seize, grasp, capture

m-ḫt when, after

msw children

mswt birth

mš' soldier

, *mk* behold; rare substitute for *ḥr* in Pseudo-verbal Construction

, *mdw* speak

mdwt disputes, words

n

n negative word

n of, to; formative element in *sḏm.n.f*

n us, we, our (suffix-pronoun)

n3 these

nỉwt city

nỉ travel; *nỉ m ḫd* sail downstream, northwards

nb every, any, all

, *nb* lord

nbw gold

nbty the Two Ladies (see p. 149)

, *nfr* good, beautiful, happy

nfrw beauty

nfrt beautiful woman

(ỉ)n-m who?

nn negative word

nḥḥ eternity

nḥḥ forever

nḥsy Nubian

nḫt mighty, strong

n-sy belong (see p. 38)

𓊨 *nsw* king

nsw-bit King of Upper and Lower Egypt

〰〰 *n-sp* together

nt of (f.)

ntf he (independent pronoun)

nṯr divine

nṯr god; *nṯr niwty* local god

, *nṯrt* goddess

nḏs little man, fellow

r

◯ *r* at, to; followed by *ḏr* plus suffix pronoun: whole; *nb/nbt r-ḏr* Lord/Lady of the Universe (e.g. *nbt r-ḏr*)

r mouth

r spell

⊙ *rʿ* Re

⊙ *rʿ* sun

r-pr temple

rn name

rḫ know, learn

ršy southern

ršyt south

ršw rejoice

ršwt joy

rṯnw Rethenu (part of Syria)

rd foot

rdi give, install; with following *sdm.f:* cause

h

h3i go, go down; with *r* to

hy husband

ḥ

ḥ3k sack

ḥ3kwt plunder

ḥ3t: m ḥ3t in the front of

ḥ3ty-ʿ count, nobleman

ḥ3t sp regnal year

ḥw O (vocative)

ḥwt-wʿrt Avaris (lit: the Mansion of the Leg)

ḥwt-nṯr temple

ḥb festival; m ḥb joyful (lit: in festival)

ḥp Inundation God (Hapy)

ḥf3w snake

ḥm majesty

ḥm servant

ḥm-nṯr priest (i.e. servant of the god)

ḥmsỉ sit, sit down; with ḥr besiege

ḥmt wife

ḥnʿ (together) with

ḥr at, in, on, upon; for use in Pseudo-verbal Construction, see p. 100; ḥr . . . ḥr . . . upon . . .

ḥr Horus

ḥryt which is on

ḥr nbw Golden Horus (see p. 149)

ḥrt: m ḥrt by land

ḥḥ Heh (place name)

ḥḥy seek

ḥknw oil

ḥk3 ruler

ḥk3t rulership

ḥkr be hungry

ḥst praise

𓏲𓊵𓏏𓊪 , 𓏲𓊵𓏏𓊪𓏥 *ḥtpw-nṯr* (god's) offerings

𓊵𓏏𓊪 *ḥtpt* offering

𓄁𓏤𓏥 *ḥḏ* silver

ẖ

𓈉 *ḫ3st* foreign land

𓈍 , 𓈍 *ḫʻı͗* rise (of sun), shine, appear in glory (of king)

𓈍 , 𓈍𓏤𓏥 *ḫʻw* weapons

𓆣 , 𓆥 *ḫpr* become, come into being

𓆣 *ḫpr* form, shape

𓆣𓀜𓂡 *ḫfʻ* fight, make a captive

𓆑𓏏 *ḫft* according as, when

𓆊𓈖𓈖 *ḫmn* not to know

𓏃𓏏𓏏𓏏 *ḫnt: r ḫnt* in front

𓏃𓏏𓏏𓏏𓈖𓏭 *ḫnty* who is at the head of, foremost

𓐍 *ḫr* under; see General Index under Auxiliary Verbs

𓏤𓄿𓐍 *ḫrw* voice

𓐍𓂋𓊪 *ḫrp* control

𓐍𓂋𓊪 *ḫsbd* lapis lazuli

𓐍𓏏 *ḫt* property

𓐍𓏏 *ḫt* thing

𓐍�End𓂃 *ḫdı͗* sail/travel downstream, northwards

ẖ

𓄚𓈖𓅱 *ẖnw: m-ẖnw* in

𓄚𓂋 *ẖr* with

𓂋𓄚𓇳 *ẖr(t)-nṯr* necropolis

𓄡𓂋� *ẖrd* child

𓄡𓏏 *ẖt* belly, body

s

𓊪 *s* her, she (suffix-pronoun)

𓀀 , 𓀁 , 𓂸 *s* man; anyone

𓀔𓏏 , 𓅭𓏏 *s3* son

𓀔𓏏𓀀 *s3w* guard

𓅭𓏏𓇳 *s3 rꜥ* son of Re

𓅭𓏏𓆇 *s3t* daughter

𓊪𓏥 *sy* her (dependent pronoun)

𓤲𓅱 *sw* he, him (dependent pronoun)

𓇳 *sw* day

𓊚 *sw3* pass; with *ḥr* pass by

𓤲𓅱𓂝 *swt* but

𓊪𓅱𓂝𓅱𓂝𓂻 *swtwt* ride abroad

𓊪𓏭𓊃𓉐 , 𓊪𓏭𓊃𓉐 *sb3* door, gate

𓊃𓊃𓀀 *sb3* teach

𓇺𓏥 *sp 2* instruction to repeat a phrase

𓊪𓅓𓇋 *smỉ* report (verb)

𓊪𓅓𓇋𓅱𓀁 *smỉw* report (noun)

𓊪𓄄𓅱𓀁 *sm3ꜥ-ḥrw* make triumphant

𓊪𓂓𓊪𓅱𓀀 *smsw* elder, eldest

𓈖𓏺 *sn* kiss

𓊪𓏤𓏤𓏤 *sn* their, they, them (suffix-pronoun)

𓊪 *snb* health

𓏏𓏭 *sn-nw* second, other;   *ḥr snnw-sy* yet again

𓊪𓈖𓏏 *snt* sister

𓊃𓈖𓇾 *sn-t3* smell

𓊪𓂋𓆓𓅓 *snḏm* rest

𓊪𓇋𓅓𓂧𓏜 *srwd* maintain

𓊪𓐍𓂓𓀀 *sḫ3* remember

𓊪𓐍𓆑𓀀 *sḫsf* create opposition

𓊃𓊃𓀀 *ss* ashes

𓊪𓊪𓂻𓂡 *sspd* make ready

𓊪𓄖𓏭𓀏𓏏𓊮 *skꜣ-ꜥnḫ* living captive

𓊪𓂆 *st* it (dependent pronoun)

𓊨𓊌 *st* place

𓊨𓎡𓏏𓁐 *st-ḥmt* woman

𓄿𓂋 *sḏm* hear, listen, understand; with *ḥr* obey

𓊪𓋬𓂡 *sḏr* spend the night

š

𓊽𓊪𓊪, 𓏏𓊪 *špss* splendid, noble

𓈙𓆑𓂧𓍱 *šfdw* book

𓈙𓄿𓂻 *šm* go, go down

𓈙𓈖 *šmw* summer

𓈙𓂋𓂻 *šms* accompany, follow

ḳ

𓂧𓏤𓄂 *ḳb* double

𓈖𓏏𓂝 *ḳnꜣ* brave

𓈖𓏏𓂾 *ḳnt* valour

k

𓎡 *k* you, your (suffix-pronoun)

𓂓 *kꜣ* soul, spirit

𓎡𓄞𓏥 *kꜣꜣ: m kꜣꜣ* by boat

𓂓𓆟 *kꜣt* work

𓎡 𓄞𓆟 *kwꜣ* Stative 1st person singular

𓎡𓄞𓆟 *kmt* Egypt

g

𓅠𓄞 *gm* find

𓎼𓂋𓎼 *grg* equip, prepare

𓎼𓂋𓏏 *grt* now

t

𓏏 *t* bread

𓇿 *t3* the (f.)

𓇾 *t3* land

𓇿𓇿 *t3wy* the Two Lands (Egypt)

𓈖𓄿𓇾𓏤𓈉 , 𓇾𓄿𓇾𓈉 *t3š* boundary

𓍿𓇋 *tỉ* Stative 2nd person c. and 3rd person f.

𓏏𓅱 *tw* impersonal pronoun (one; One when referring to king); passive element

𓏏𓅱𓏏𓀾 *twt* image, statue

𓁶 *tp* head, person; upon: 𓁶𓈋𓆑 *tp dw.f* who is upon his mountain

𓁷 *tpy* first

𓏏𓅓𓀜 *tm* negative verb

𓏏𓈖 *tn* this (f.)

t̲

𓍿 *t̲* you, your (suffix-pronoun)

𓏲𓅱 *t̲3w* breath

𓏏𓈖 *t̲n* your, yourselves (suffix-pronoun)

d

𓂞 , 𓄿 *dỉ* give

𓇼𓇳 *dw3* morning

𓇼𓅱𓇳 *dw3w* dawn, morning; *m dw3(w)* tomorrow

𓊠𓊡 *dpt* boat

𓂧𓏤𓏏 *dmỉ* habitation

𓂧𓏤𓏏 , 𓂧𓏤𓏏 *dmỉ* town

𓂧𓏤𓏏 *dmỉ* touch

𓂦𓏤 *dmd̲ r* total

𓂧𓂋𓀜 *dr* drive out, subdue

𓂧𓂋𓏏𓂝 *drt* hand

𓂧𓉔𓈖 *dhn* promote

_ḏ_

🔵🔵🔵 _ḏꜣi̯_ cross, ferry across

🔵🔵🔵 _ḏw_ bad, evil

🔵_ḏr: r ḏr.(f)_ whole, entire (see p. 17)

🔵 _ḏḥwty_ Thoth

🔵 _ḏs_ self (see p. 32)

🔵 _ḏt_ forever

🔵 _ḏd_ say, speak, tell

🔵 _ḏd_ stability

🔵🔵🔵🔵 _ḏdkw_ Djedeku (name of a canal at Avaris)

FURTHER READING

A. Blackman, '*Middle Egyptian stories*', Brussels, 1932. (see p. 41 ff for complete *hieroglyphic* text of 'The Shipwrecked Sailor').

A. Erman, '*The Ancient Egyptians; a sourcebook of their writings*', Harper Torchbooks, N.Y., 1966. (see p. 29 ff for a translation of 'The Shipwrecked Sailor').

R. O. Faulkner, '*A concise dictionary of Middle Egyptian*', O.U.P. Oxford, 1964.

Sir Alan Gardiner, '*Egyptian grammar*', 3rd ed., O.U.P., London, 1966.

S. Shennum, '*English-Egyptian index of Faulkner's "Concise dictionary of Middle Egyptian"* ', Malibu, 1977.

GENERAL INDEX